The Assyrian Empire

An Enthralling Overview of the History of Assyria, the Assyrians, and Their Role in Ancient Mesopotamia

© Copyright 2024 - All rights reserved.

The content contained within this book may not be reproduced, duplicated, or transmitted without direct written permission from the author or the publisher.

Under no circumstances will any blame or legal responsibility be held against the publisher, or author, for any damages, reparation, or monetary loss due to the information contained within this book, either directly or indirectly.

Legal Notice:

This book is copyright protected. It is only for personal use. You cannot amend, distribute, sell, use, quote, or paraphrase any part, or the content within this book, without the consent of the author or publisher.

Disclaimer Notice:

Please note the information contained within this document is for educational and entertainment purposes only. All effort has been executed to present accurate, up-to-date, reliable, and complete information. No warranties of any kind are declared or implied. Readers acknowledge that the author is not engaging in the rendering of legal, financial, medical, or professional advice. The content within this book has been derived from various sources. Please consult a licensed professional before attempting any techniques outlined in this book.

By reading this document, the reader agrees that under no circumstances is the author responsible for any losses, direct or indirect, that are incurred as a result of the use of the information contained within this document, including, but not limited to, errors, omissions, or inaccuracies.

Free limited time bonus

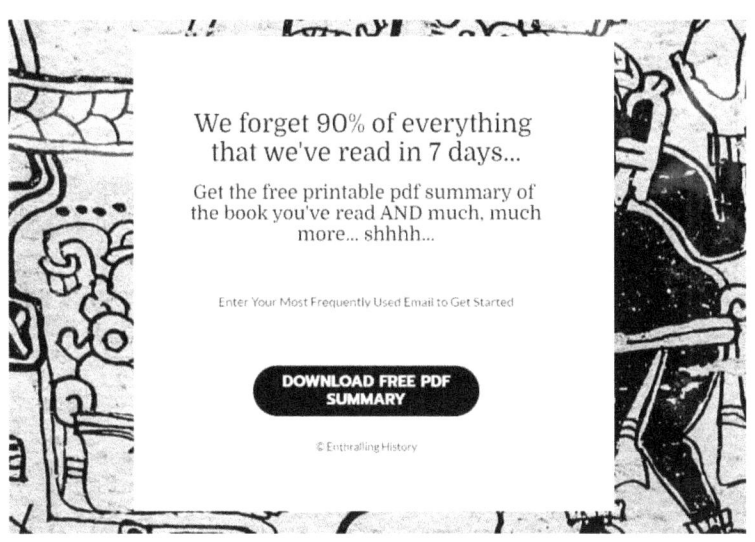

Stop for a moment. We have a free bonus set up for you. The problem is this: we forget 90% of everything that we read after 7 days. Crazy fact, right? Here's the solution: we've created a printable, 1-page pdf summary for this book that you're reading now. All you have to do to get your free pdf summary is to go to the following website: https://livetolearn.lpages.co/enthrallinghistory/

Or, Scan the QR code!

Once you do, it will be intuitive. Enjoy, and thank you!

Table of Contents

INTRODUCTION 1
CHAPTER 1: NORTH MESOPOTAMIA BEFORE THE ASSYRIANS 10
CHAPTER 2: THE EARLY PERIOD AND THE AKKADIAN EMPIRE 20
CHAPTER 3: THE OLD ASSYRIAN EMPIRE AND BABYLON 27
CHAPTER 4: RESTORATION AND FALL TO THE MITANNI 36
CHAPTER 5: THE MIDDLE ASSYRIAN EMPIRE 39
CHAPTER 6: ASSYRIA DURING THE BRONZE AGE COLLAPSE 44
CHAPTER 7: THE NEO-ASSYRIAN EMPIRE... 47
CHAPTER 8: LANGUAGE DIVERSITY 74
CHAPTER 9: RELIGION AND BELIEFS 80
CHAPTER 10: ARTS AND ARCHITECTURE... 88
CONCLUSION 96
HERE'S ANOTHER BOOK BY ENTHRALLING HISTORY THAT YOU MIGHT LIKE.. 99
FREE LIMITED TIME BONUS 100
BIBLIOGRAPHY 101
IMAGE SOURCES 103

Introduction

Assyria was one of the world's first great powers. It was based in northern Mesopotamia—the area between the rivers Tigris and Euphrates in modern Iraq. Assyria started out as one of a number of Middle Eastern states, but it rapidly became one of the most influential. Eventually, after a series of conquests, it became one of the world's first empires. It included not just its heartland in modern Iraq but also parts of Syria, Turkey, Lebanon, Iran, Israel, and Jordan.

It's fascinating to find out how the process of state formation worked in ancient times. It's even more fascinating that when this empire failed, it failed catastrophically and quickly. It went from riches to rags in a single generation.

However, until fairly recently, Assyria was hardly known at all, apart from a few biblical references. It was only in the mid-19th century that archaeologists started discovering the early civilizations of Mesopotamia.

Austen Henry Layard was the first to start excavations, concentrating on Nineveh, King Sennacherib's capital. He also worked at Nimrud (ancient Kalhu) and later on Babylonian sites in the south of Mesopotamia. He published the first works on Assyria and sent a large number of antiquities to the British Museum. As well as uncovering splendid palaces, massive sculptures, and delicate friezes, he also found an amazing resource, the Library of Ashurbanipal. This consisted of twenty-two thousand inscribed clay tablets dating from around 668 to 627 BCE and covered the history of Assyria and earlier cultures, going back two thousand years from Ashurbanipal's time.

However, Layard did not excavate at Ashur, the original Assyrian capital. This excavation had to wait until 1903 for German archaeologist Walter Andrae, who spent eleven years excavating the site. He was a more systematic archaeologist than Layard. Andrae dug trenches across the entire site to understand the life and layout of the city, including small houses, temples, and palaces.

Assyria was not the first civilization in the Middle East. The Sumerians ruled for several centuries before the rise of Assyria. The Sumerian culture was preserved as a "classical" culture by the Assyrians. And from the very beginning of Assyria, there was a deep rivalry with Babylon, which was based in the more fertile lands farther south.

Although Assyria was not the first empire, it lasted much longer than the Akkadian Empire. And thanks to the preservation of its libraries, we know a lot about it. We know how production was centralized and controlled, what happened in the temples, what omens were considered good (and what was unlikely), and what food was considered a particular delicacy (locusts).

This book will cover Assyrian history from the very beginning to the end of the empire. First, it will introduce the Sumerians, who developed many of the technologies and ideologies the Assyrians used to create their state, and the Akkadians, who were the first real military power in Mesopotamia. The Assyrians knew their history, as some Assyrian kings even took Akkadian kings' names, perhaps stressing their desire to emulate Akkadian success in war.

The Assyrians had a reputation for being a particularly aggressive nation. This was partly because they were, for centuries, known only through the Bible, where they were shown as warlike aggressors. The poet Lord Byron certainly saw them this way:

"The Assyrian came down like a wolf on the fold,

And his cohorts were gleaming in purple and gold;

And the sheen of their spears was like stars on the sea,

When the blue wave rolls nightly on deep Galilee." - Lord Byron[i]

Of course, there was more to Assyrian expansion than just military prowess. Little by little, the Assyrians built an empire rather than just an assemblage of conquered states. To do that, they had to innovate

---

[i] Lord Byron, "The Destruction of Sennacherib" lines 1-4, from *Hebrew Melodies*, 1815.

economically and create a highly structured administration and infrastructure, such as roads and a post office.

There are a few difficulties in writing Assyrian history. Some early kings (not listed in the timeline below) are only known from lists of Assyrian kings that were written much later; they may be mythical. Dating is not reliable for the Old and Middle Assyrian periods. For the early era, most of the data historians can use is known through royal inscriptions in temples, which were intended to show the king as an ideal ruler, building cities and temples, defeating enemies, and producing plenty of sacrifices for the gods. They are, obviously, biased. The Neo-Assyrian Empire has detailed correspondence that allows for a clearer assessment of rulers as individuals, and even then, it is sometimes not quite clear why certain things happened or exactly what happened.

Correspondence between merchants and traders exists from earlier periods that give us a fascinating view of the life of the middle classes at the time. Many of these letters were found in the houses of the individuals concerned in the letter, so the archaeological and written evidence complement each other in an unusual and very satisfying way.

Understanding the Assyrians just in terms of names and dates doesn't give the whole picture. That's why this book includes chapters on the languages they used, their art and superb monumental architecture, and their religion. While, in some ways, the Assyrians can seem quite close to us (they loved their beer, for instance), in other ways, their culture was very different (for instance, they lived on top of their ancestors' tombs or used oracles to decide military strategy).

An impression of what Nineveh might have looked like at its height.[1]

Assyria might not have been where you'd want to live. It certainly wasn't an empire you would want to fight. Nevertheless, it left some magnificent remains behind, and for many Assyrians, including subject peoples, life was good, not least because one of the avowed tasks of any Assyrian king was to look after his people's well-being.

It's well worth studying the Assyrians since their idea of how to put a state together became incredibly influential over the next several hundred years. Without Assyria, there would have been no Persian Empire, no Alexander the Great, and no Roman Empire. And without the Romans, Western history would have looked very different.

Timeline

Old Assyrian Period	
Puzur-Ashur I	C2025 BCE
Shalim-ahum	uncertain
Ilu-Shuma	uncertain
Erishum I	1974-1935 BCE
Ikunum	1934-1921
Sargon I	1920-1881
Puzur-Ashur II	1880-1873
Naram-Sin	1872-1819
Erishum II	1818-1809
Shamsi-Adad	
Shamshi-Adad I	1808-1776

Ishme-Dagan I	1775-1765
Mut-Ashkur	uncertain
Rimush	uncertain
Asinum	uncertain
Usurpers 1735-1701	
Puzur-Sin	
Ashur-dugul	
Ashur-apla-idi	
Nasir-Sin	
Sin-namir	
Ipqi-Ishtar	
Adad-Salulu	
Adasi	
Adasides	
Bel-bani	1700-1691
Libaya	1690-1674
Sharma-Adad I	1673-1662
Iptar-Sin	1661-1650

Bazaya	1649-1622
Lullaya	1621-1616
Shu-Ninua	1615-1602
Sharma-Adad II	1601-1599
Erishum III	1598-1586
Shamshi-Adad II	1585-1580
Ishme-Dagan II	1579-1564
Shamshi-Adad III	1563-1548
Ashur-nirari I	1547-1522
Puzur-Ashur III	1521-1498
Enlil-nasir I	1497-1485
Nur-ili	1484-1473
Ashur-shaduni	1473
Ashur-rabi I	1472-1453
Ashur-nadin-ahhe I	1452-1431
Enlil-nasir II	1430-1425
Ashur-nirari II	1424-1418
Ashur-bel-nisheshu	1417-1409

Ashur-rim-nisheshu	1408-1401
Ashur-nadin-ahhe II	1400-1391
Eriba-Adad I	1390-1364
Middle Assyrian Period	
Ashur-uballit I	1363-1328
Enlil-nirari	1327-1318
Arik-den-ili	1317-1306
Adad-nirari I	1305-1274
Shalmaneser I	1273-1244
Tukulti-Ninurta I	1243-1207
Ashur-nadin-apli	1206-1203
Ashur-nirari III	1202-1197
Enlil-kudurri-usur	1196-1192
Ninurta-apal-Ekur	1191-1179
Ashur-Dan I	1178-1133
Ninurta-tukulti-Ashur	1132
Mutakkil-Nusku	1132
Ashur-resh-ishi I	1132-1115

Tiglath-Pileser I	1114-1076
Asharid-apal-Ekur	1075-1074
Ashur-bel-kala	1073-1056
Eriba-Adad II	1055-1054
Shamshi-Adad IV	1053-1050
Ashurnasirpal I	1049-1031
Shalmaneser II	1030-1019
Ashur-nirari IV	1018-1013
Ashur-rabi II	1012-972
Ashur-resh-ishi II	971-967
Tiglath-Pileser II	966-935
Ashur-Dan II	934-912
Neo-Assyrian Empire	
Adad-nirari II	911-891
Tukulti-Ninurta II	890-884
Ashurnasirpal II	883-859
Shalmaneser III	859-824
Shamshi-Adad V	824-811

Adad-nirari III	811-783
Shalmaneser IV	783-773
Ashur-Dan III	773-755
Ashur-nirari V	755-745
Tiglath-Pileser III	745-727
Shalmaneser V	727-722
Sargonids	
Sargon II	722-705
Sennacherib	705-681
Esarhaddon	681-669
Ashurbanipal	669-631
Ashur-etil-ilani	631-627
Sin-sumu-lisir	626
Sinsharishkun	627-612
Ashur-uballit II	612-609

Note: All of these regnal years are approximate dates; it is impossible to know for sure when all these kings ruled. Also, the Mesopotamian practice was to date a king's rule from his first full year in office rather than from his accession. That's why the dates for many kings in the earlier periods look too neat. For the later part of the Neo-Assyrian Empire, more detailed information allows for more precise dating.

Chapter 1: North Mesopotamia Before the Assyrians

Mesopotamia is known as the land "between the rivers" (that's what the name means in Greek). The rivers in question were the Euphrates and the Tigris, which ran down through what is now Iraq toward the Persian Gulf.

Mesopotamia was mainly flat land, steppes, plains, and marshland. Particularly toward the south, there was a lot of fertile soil with a lot of silt and clay. However, the conditions were arid, and toward the sea, the land is very marshy, so a certain amount of hard work was required to make the land productive.

Civilization emerged first in Mesopotamia, even before it did in Egypt, the Indus Valley, or China. The first people in the area were the Proto-Euphrateans or Ubaid people, Stone Age agriculturalists living in small villages whose settlements have since been excavated at al-Ubaid, near Ur. However, it wasn't until the Sumerians arrived, possibly from somewhere near the Caspian Sea, that an urban culture was first created.

A map of Mesopotamia showing some of the early settlement sites.[2]

The Sumerians made huge advances. They advanced from the Stone Age (Chalcolithic, to be precise) into the Bronze Age and vastly increased agricultural productivity through irrigation. They also invented the seeder plow, which had a funnel to place the seed immediately after the furrow had been turned. This was much more efficient than simply throwing the seed (known as broadcast sowing) and might have increased yields by as much as 50 percent.

Sumer didn't just have a singular water god. The main water god's name was Enki, who is often shown with the two great rivers falling from his shoulders like watery wings. There was also a canal god, Ennugi. Everything in Sumer came from the rivers. The rivers gave them water for agriculture, fish, clay for pottery, bundles of reeds tied together for the earliest buildings, and clay for mudbricks.

The Sumerians also told the story of a great flood, similar to that of Noah's flood. Both the Tigris and the Euphrates overflowed frequently but also unpredictably, and the myth reflects that reality. This flooding made Mesopotamia a different place from Egypt, where the overflowing of the Nile was predictable; the Egyptian civilization developed in a very different way because of that.

There's another link to the Great Flood too. The Bible sets out the way in which Noah was the patriarch of all the people of the Middle East. According to the Bible, Noah's three sons each began a family of nations. Shem, for instance, was the father of the Hebrews, but his sons also included Elam, founder of the Iranian city-state of Elam, and Ashur, founder of the city of Ashur and the Assyrian nation. Ham's family founded Egypt and the Canaanite culture. Ham's grandson, Nimrod, was later traditionally identified as the builder of the Tower of Babel.

However, the Bible obviously doesn't mention the fact that Ashur was not a king but a deity, and Nimrod is not attested in any of the king lists of Babylon.

The first writing and mathematics are found in Sumer. Writing started as rough pictographs, originating around 3000 BCE. It soon developed into a more abstract script written on clay found in the river basin. Writing enabled the Sumerians to write down a code of law for the first time in human history. Written law played a big part in Sumerian society; for example, deeds of sale have been found dating from 2700 BCE onward.

For arithmetic, Sumerians used base six as well as base ten. The need to account for agricultural surpluses might have motivated the development of both math and writing. The transition to a money economy also happened at an early date. (It's interesting that Egypt didn't develop a money economy for two millennia; it developed a centralized economy rather than a commercial one.) Perhaps it's significant that math questions for pupils reflected their concern with water resources and agriculture. "If a cistern measures this wide and this deep, and it's full, how much land can it irrigate?" seems to have been a typical way of exercising young students' minds.

Reliance on irrigation also meant that Sumer needed a method of organizing its population and land holdings to enable large irrigation systems to be set up. In other words, the need to irrigate forced the state to evolve. Urban living also required a more complex system of governance than pastoralism, which led to increasing specialization of crafts. Rather than living in small settlements, Sumerians set up cities, which were walled very early on.

There was one major problem, though. Mesopotamia had rivers, silt, and clay. What it didn't have a lot of was metal, stone, and wood. There were no major metal resources in the region, and trees didn't grow well there. This forced Sumer to trade its agricultural surplus for everything it required. By the time the Sumerian civilization had matured, the Sumerian cities were trading as far afield as India, the Horn of Africa, and the Caspian and Mediterranean Seas.

Yet, for a very long time, all trace of Sumer was lost. It was even better hidden than Assyria since it wasn't mentioned in the Bible. Although first Old Persian, Assyrian, and Babylonian cuneiform texts had been deciphered, Sumerian took longer. It wasn't until 1869 that French Assyriologist Jules Oppert named the writers of the early cuneiform as Sumerians. The excavation of Sumerian Lagash in 1877 and the excavation of Nippur vastly expanded the number of texts in Sumerian available to scholars.

Sir Leonard Woolley made the next big advances in the 1920s and 1930s when he excavated Uruk and then Ur. At Ur, he found the tomb of Queen Pu-Abi, an untouched royal tomb containing a cylindrical seal with her name on it, a golden headdress, a chariot, and a harp. He also discovered a number of other tombs and death pits containing the bodies of retainers who appear to have been sacrificed.

These excavations, together with the use of Sumerian written texts, enable archaeological stratigraphy (dating artifacts by the layers, or strata, of the earth in which they are found) to be cross-checked against Sumerian records. The dating of Sumerian history is based on archaeologists' discoveries in Uruk, where a twenty-meter-deep test pit enabled archaeologists to determine the stratigraphy from the first settlement on the site to about 2500 BCE, by which time the Sumerians were already using writing.

Around one thousand "historical" inscriptions from Sumer survive, but date formulas used in administrative and commercial documents can also be used to help date events. Years were not numbered; rather, they were named after particularly important events that occurred, and lists were then created of the year names for each king's reign.

The Sumerian King List, of which sixteen versions (mostly incomplete) survive, runs from the line "after the kingship descended from heaven, the kingship was in the city of Eridu" to the historical Isin dynasty. The history of Sumer probably began between 4500 and 4000 BCE when the first settlements were established. The Sumerian culture lasted nearly three thousand years from this date.

The king list is based on the idea that "kingship" was invested in one city at a time. After the Great Flood, first Kish, then Uruk, and then Ur are mentioned as sites of kingship, giving the impression that each succeeded the other. In fact, these dynasties overlapped, with all three cities competing for dominance. Other cities that are noted in the king list are Akshak, Mari, Adab, and Lagash.

There were around a dozen city-states in Sumer. Each was a walled city and had a ziggurat—Sumer's biggest contribution to architecture. A ziggurat is a sort of stepped pyramid, which perhaps began as a square plinth or mound under a temple building. More terraces were added around this; the center was made of relatively soft, unfired mudbricks, which was then surrounded by retaining walls made of fired (harder) mudbricks. (The Ziggurat in West Sacramento, California, is an excellent model; the SIS Building in London, England, is a flashier update.)

The Great Ziggurat of Ur[8]

The earliest ziggurat dates from around 4000 BCE, but its precursors were raised platforms or mounds dating from as far back as the Ubaid period in the 6th millennium BCE. The ziggurat was seen as a means of connecting heaven and earth. Babylon's ziggurat was called Etemenanki,

"House of the Foundation of Heaven and Earth" in Sumerian.

On flat land, builders made an artificial mountain on top of which the city's deity was thought to live. Ziggurats were part of a sacred complex that included other buildings, and they were the tallest buildings in each city. According to Herodotus, there was a shrine at the top of each ziggurat. None have ever been found, but the advanced state of ruination of most extant ziggurats may account for that. Ziggurats were not public places; they were the dwelling places of the gods. Only priests would have had access in order to provide the gods with food and drink and otherwise care for them.

Every city had its own god, something that became very important once Assyria started to build an empire. Babylon's god was Marduk, Uruk's deity was the goddess Inanna, and Enlil, the earth god, was the patron of Nippur.

It seems that Sumerian cities were not initially ruled by kings but run by an *ensi*, or governor, in cooperation with a council. Kingship probably grew out of the need for military leadership once the city-states started to compete with each other.

It's intriguing that in most Sumerian cities, there is a distinct separation between the temple and the palace. Both are placed at the edge of the city, but they are distant from each other. However, the temple always seems to have dominated the skyline.

One thing that was very important to the Sumerians was beer; this was a Mesopotamian passion that continued under the Assyrians and Babylonians. In fact, the Sumerians probably invented beer. They gave it a goddess, Ninkasi, whose name means "mistress of beer." Beer was usually drunk through a long straw so several people could drink from the same pot at once, which was a great way to promote friendship and cooperation among the people.

You may not think beer is historically important, but one of the very few inscriptions that mention King Enannatum II of Lagash is an inscription on the door socket of Nigirsu's brewery, telling how Enannatum, son of Entemena, ensi of Lagash, restored the brewery for the warrior god Nigursu. Without that brewery, it might not have been possible to distinguish him from Enannatum I, and history would look just a tiny bit different.

Uruk was the first great city. It is called Erech in the Bible or Warka in Arabic. Its first king was Meskiaggasher, and he was followed by his son Enmerkar. Then, his companion, Lugalbanda, took the throne, and Dumuzi followed him. Dumuzi became the focus of a sacred marriage rite and formal mourning once he died. These rites were still being celebrated in the 6th century BCE). The next king, according to the Sumerian King List, was Gilgamesh, who became the Sumerian hero par excellence. He ruled Uruk between 2900 and 2350 BCE during the Early Dynastic period.

The *Epic of Gilgamesh* was one of the texts discovered in the Library of Ashurbanipal. It tells how the hero Gilgamesh befriends the wild man Enkidu, how together they defeat Humbaba, and how Gilgamesh rejects the goddess Ishtar and defeats the Bull of Heaven, which she sends to punish him for his rejection. Then, Enkidu dies, and Gilgamesh, afraid of death, tries to find immortality. He fails in his quest, but he returns to Uruk, understanding that he, too, will die (not the most upbeat of endings, it has to be said, but it does pack an emotional punch that even modern-day humans can understand).

Although the *Epic of Gilgamesh* is written in Akkadian and was probably written between 1600 and 1100 BCE, long after the end of Sumerian rule, the Akkadian text conflated several different Sumerian texts, which still exist, each telling a different episode of the story. Gilgamesh is also attested by more prosaic inscriptions as a historical figure. A very early inscription states, "Gilgamesh is the one selected by Utu [the sun god]," and the Tummal Inscription, which dates to around 1950 BCE, credits him with rebuilding the walls of Uruk, which were nearly six miles long.

Uruk was a key cult center for the goddess Ishtar or Inanna. In fact, the development of the city might have been driven by its priesthood rather than its kings. The temple seems to have been built before any palaces. The king's relationship to the gods was crucial. It was believed that the gods chose the king, giving him divine approval, but the king needed to continue to ensure the gods' support by enriching the temples. Unlike in ancient Egypt, the king himself was not seen as divine—hence Gilgamesh's struggles with mortality.

Uruk was a sizable city. At its prime, it might have had as many as 100,000 people, not far off from the population of Albany, New York, or Wichita Falls, Texas, today.

Ashur, the city that lent its name to the Assyrians, was probably founded around 2600 BCE, by which time Uruk was already a mature and highly populated city. During its early years, Ashur was sometimes independent. At other times, it was subject to Akkad or Ur.

Ashur was situated just at the edge of the fertile zone, where there would have been enough rainfall for agriculture. Even so, agriculture around Ashur was marginal, with low yields compared to the south. Agriculture here was fed by rain. In Babylonia, to the south, the rivers delivered most of the water through irrigation canals. Since it was hard to grow enough agriculture to feed the inhabitants of Ashur, trade became a pressing concern. Tin, a necessary ingredient for making bronze, came from central Asia, while copper came from Anatolia. Silver, which was the main currency of the Middle East at the time (not gold), also came from Anatolia. Throughout Assyria's history, securing supplies of timber and metal drove expansionist policies. In its earliest days, Ashur became a major commercial center.

Why build a city in a less fertile area? The answer is likely the fact that the site controlled a ford on the Tigris, which opened up trade routes to Syria, Anatolia, and central Asia. The site also had a huge rock outcrop above the river, which made it defensible. On open land with no clear natural boundaries, cities were open to attack by nomads coming down from the highlands, so Ashur's craggy site was a key strategic advantage.

Ashur was a liminal spot, the threshold between the fertile land and the arid land to the west, where nomadic herdsmen relied on pastoralism as a way of life. The heartlands of Assyria were always to the east of Ashur, roughly in a triangle between the cities of Nineveh, Arbela, and Ashur.

Tin, a necessary ingredient for making bronze, came from Central Asia, while copper came from Anatolia, as did silver, which was the main currency of the Middle East at the time (not gold).

Ashur was situated on a tight bend of the Tigris River, where a forty-meter rocky outcrop now called Qal'at Sherqat soars above the river. This rock was the site of Ashur's temple, and it's likely that the rock itself was originally seen as embodying the deity. The god and the city would have been one and the same thing to the Assyrians. At various times, this temple was given different names in the Sumerian language:

- Eamkurkurra - the house of the wild bull of the lands
- Ehursagkurkurra - the house of the mountain of the lands
- Esharra - the house of the universe.

The Sumerian economy was a mixed model. The temples controlled a good deal of the wealth, as did the nobility, but there was also a middle class to which many of the merchants belonged. Slavery existed. Most slaves were prisoners of war, but debtors could also be enslaved by their creditors, and some parents sold their children in time of need. However, slaves could buy their freedom, and any child who had a free father was born free.

Monogamy was the usual practice unless the first wife had no children. Male and female spheres became sharply defined over time. There might have been female rulers very early on (probably priestesses ruling a temple-led culture), but by the later period, kings were exclusively male. However, women could run their own businesses. They could also buy and sell land and slaves. They were often bakers, brewers, and weavers.

Kingship "descended from heaven," as it says in the Sumerian King List. The king was the representative of the gods. He was responsible for "feeding" the gods, protecting the city against its enemies, and establishing justice. Images of the king frequently show him as a provider, sacrificing to a god, building a temple, making a libation (pouring out beer on the ground), or hosting a banquet. (The word "banquet," by the way, is literally "pouring out beer" in Sumerian.)

Kings are also shown as protectors. For instance, there are scenes of kings fighting or killing lions, which became a prevalent image in the area from the Sumerians all the way to the end of the Assyrian Empire. The king is often seen in triumph, driving his chariot, reviewing prisoners of war, or presenting his captives to the gods, but there is no equivalent to the "smiting scene" in Egyptian culture, which shows the pharaoh grabbing enemies by the hair and raising his mace to smash their heads.

Kings in Sumer were often called the "beloved of Inanna." However, scholars have disagreed on how to interpret the concept of sacred marriage. Royal hymns of Ur-Namma from the Neo-Sumerian period refer to a sexual union between Inanna and the ruler. Some have suggested that the king was initiated by a priestess of Inanna's temple, while others believe the image was simply a metaphor. The scene of the king watering a tiny palm tree in a pot might have been a sophisticated metaphor for the sacred marriage (water and semen are referred to by the same word in Sumerian, "a").

Sumerian culture was highly literate, not just in terms of being able to read and write but also in terms of reverence for the written word. Every building had a foundation tablet inscribed and buried. Words were a form of magic; it was as if writing something down could make it happen. When a king rebuilt a temple, he would try to find the foundation tablets that the first builder and any subsequent restorers had deposited. He would make sacrifices, oil the tablets, and then place them with a new tablet that recorded the restoration. The tablets were, in a way, sacred objects, preserving the lineage of the royal family and the history of the temple.

There is a great deal of continuity between the Sumerians and the civilizations that succeeded them. However, there was also a major break in history, as new people speaking a different language arrived in Mesopotamia and set up their own civilization. That is the subject of the next chapter.

Chapter 2: The Early Period and the Akkadian Empire

Around 2800 BCE or a little later, a number of new people started to arrive in Mesopotamia. Unlike the Sumerians, they spoke a Semitic language, an ancestor of modern Arabic. (Nineteenth-century archaeologists saw the racial question as highly important, and they contrasted Sumer and the Semitic "races" of Babylon and Assyria. In fact, Mesopotamia appears to have been a highly unified, multi-lingual culture. The Sumerian language survived and was used alongside the Semitic languages of Babylonian and Assyrian. Sumerian-language texts were sometimes signed by scribes with Akkadian names. Much of Sumerian religion and social organization survived in the later cultures too.)

While the names of the kings of Kish were Akkadian from 2800 BCE onward, the first ruler who is well attested is Sargon the Great, the first ruler of the Akkadian Empire and the founder of the Old Akkadian dynasty, which ruled for a century after his death. Sargon (Sharru-ukin in Akkadian, meaning "the king is established") came to power around 2334 BCE and brought with him a new concept of kingship and the territorial state.

During this period, there was tension between the Sumerian idea of the city-state, as new concepts of territorial states could include a number of cities. The Sumerian city-states sometimes came together and sometimes separated; their relations were often fluid. Sargon was hellbent on conquest, though. The regnal year names for his reign show the nature of his rule. They include "Year in which he destroyed Elam" and "Year in which Mari was destroyed."

Sargon's capital, Akkad or Agade, has not yet been identified. It was most likely in the area of Baghdad. Sargon himself is something of a mystery; even his name might be just his title as king rather than his birthname or adoptive name. The Sumerian King List says that he was the son of a gardener and a cup-bearer to King Ur-Zababa of Kish. The *Legend of Sargon of Akkad*, a Sumerian text, says that when Ur-Zababa heard that Sargon had dreamed of the goddess Inanna's favor, he tried to have Sargon killed. He sent Sargon to the chief smith with a bronze mirror. Ur-Zababa told the smith to throw both the mirror and Sargon into the crucible. However, Inanna warned Sargon to hand over the mirror and not to enter the workshop. So, Sargon was saved.

An Akkadian text from around 2300 BCE (contemporary with Sargon) tells how Sargon's mother put him in a basket of rushes and cast him into the river. Akki, the drawer of water, found him and decided to look after him. Sargon was Akki's gardener when the goddess Ishtar granted him her love, and he became king. (This is remarkably similar to the story of Moses, though not quite the same. Moses, after all, was brought up by the pharaoh's daughter.)

In Neo-Assyrian literature, Sargon appears as an almost legendary figure. Perhaps he could be compared to King Arthur, who might have been based on a real ruler but developed a whole mythical narrative, including the Lady of the Lake who gives Arthur a sword, an episode quite close to the narrative of Ishtar's favor and also includes water. Arthur is said to have been conceived when King Uther Pendragon disguises himself as Igraine's husband and lies with her. Sargon, on the other hand, is born of a "changeling" mother; his father is unknown. However, while historians generally don't believe Arthur existed in reality, we know that Sargon did.

Sargon's story fascinated the Assyrians. Some Assyrian rulers even adopted the Akkadian names Sargon and Naram-sin (Sargon's grandson), hoping to emulate the Sargonid dynasty's achievements.

Sargon was a military genius, but he was also a savvy administrator. He used archers and light troops rather than heavy infantry. Unlike the Sumerian states, he maintained a permanent army rather than raising levies when needed. He took Uruk and Mari, conquered Ur and

Umma, and raided Elam. Under Sargon, Sumer became unified into a single state. He conquered lands in the Levant as far north as Lebanon, which meant the Akkadian Empire stretched from the Mediterranean to the Persian Gulf. He also made Akkadian the official language.

Sargon's inscriptions and those of his sons, Rimush and Manishtushu, survive, albeit only in the form of copies made some centuries later. He was known as "Sargon, king of Akkad, overseer of Inanna, king of Kish, anointed of Anu, king of the land [Mesopotamia], governor [ensi] of Enlil." Sargon boasted that 5,400 men ate bread daily before him as members of his household. This was his administrative and military team.

With Sargon, the idea of being king changed. Sumerian kings represented themselves as *primus inter pares*, "first among equals." Gudea, ruler of Lagash, for instance, made many almost life-size statues of himself, but he appears as an ordinary man in a robe. His inscriptions don't talk about his victories. Instead, they detail his pious acts. Sargon, on the other hand, stresses his aggression and military prowess in his inscriptions. He set himself apart from other men. He certainly saw himself as the first in a line of heroic rulers.

The Mask of Sargon, now thought to represent Naram-Sin of Akkad'.

Manishtushu, Sargon's son, was succeeded by Naram-Sin of Akkad. He ruled between 2254 and 2218. Naram-Sin appears to have centralized the administration, increasing royal control of the various city-states. However, this set off a major uprising. The rulers of Kish and Uruk led the revolt, together with numerous other city-states. Then, the Gutians from the mountainous region to the east of Mesopotamia invaded, briefly conquering the whole of Sumer. Naram-Sin appears to have successfully put down the first rebellions, but later in his reign, he lost control of much of the empire.

Shar-Kali-Sharri, Naram-Sin's son, took over Akkad, but the fact that he didn't use the title "king of the four quarters" like his predecessors suggests that he realized his dominion was much less extensive than his father's. He might have been the last Akkadian king to control more than just the city of Akkad.

In 2193, the Gutians invaded again. Not much is known about the Gutians, but they threw Akkad into chaos. The Sumerian King List describes this period with the question, "Then who was king? Who was not king?" There were a number of rivals who took the throne for short periods. In 2189, the dynasty was reestablished under Dudu, who was probably the son of Shar-Kali-Sharri. Dudu's son, Shu-turul (c. 2168–2154), was the last king of Akkad. After this, Uruk regained preeminence.

Sargon's Akkadian Empire lasted less than two hundred years. This gave rise to the idea of the "Curse of Akkad." A Sumerian literary composition called *The Frown of Enlil* asserted that Akkad had fallen out of favor because its later kings disrespected the gods. Whatever happened, the Akkadian Empire retained its hold on the imaginations and ambitions of later kings. For instance, Ur-Nammu, who founded the Neo-Sumerian Empire, called himself "king of Sumer and Akkad." Assyrian kings also used the title when they held control of Babylon.

After the fall of Akkad and after some years of Gutian rule, a number of Sumerian cities were able to reassert their independence, including Ur, Uruk, Lagash, and Umma.

Gudea of Lagash, who ruled between 2080 and 2060 BCE, might have been the impetus behind this movement. He claimed several conquests, but most of his inscriptions record the creation of irrigation channels and temples. This represents a return to the Sumerian style of kingship rather than the military imperialism of Akkadian rulers.

Under Gudea, Lagash traded with Oman, northern Arabia, Lebanon, Sinai, and even India. His title was *ensi*, town leader or governor, rather than *lugal* (Sumerian) or *sharrum* (Assyrian), or king. Gudea is well known from the numerous statues he had made of himself. He is often shown with the drafts of a temple plan in his lap. He ruled for two decades, and he was later deified.

Gudea of Lagash, a statue in the Louvre. Note the writing on his apron. By the way, this is the only image of a ruler in this book that shows a non-bearded man. Both the Akkadians and the Assyrians had long hair and beards. Some Sumerians were also bearded. It may be that Gudea had to shave his beard and head because he was a priest and needed to be in a state of ritual purity.[5]

Another major ruler, Ur-Nammu, came to power in Ur at a time shortly before Gudea's reign in Lagash. He probably ruled from 2212 to 2094 and founded the Third Dynasty of Ur, which is also sometimes known as the Neo-Sumerian Empire. Ur came out ahead in a major power struggle after the Gutian invasion and extended its rule farther north.

He defeated Lagash and Uruk and was crowned at Nippur. He eventually came to rule Eridu and Susa. He was a state-builder, but he was also a ziggurat-builder, creating the Great Ziggurat of Ur. He also created a law code, the Code of Ur-Nammu, which is the first known unitary code, and standardized weights and measures.[i] But unlike the Akkadians, he was not particularly interested in conquering the north of Mesopotamia. He preferred diplomacy so that towns like Nineveh, Mari, and Ebla remained independent but were friendly to Ur.

A set of weights from Shalmaneser V's reign.[6]

Like Gudea, Ur-Nammu emphasized civil works in his inscriptions. Draining the marshes was a particularly important aspect of his work, creating more and richer farmland to feed a growing population. By this time, Ur had 200,000 people.

The Neo-Sumerian Empire also included Ashur. Several documents from Ur mention individuals with names including Ashur, so this was clearly not a Sumerian ethnic state; it included people of Akkadian and Assyrian origin.

---

[i] A set of sixteen different pweights from the time of Shalmaneser V was found at Nimrud. They were all roaring lions that could be lifted by their curved-over tails.

Ur-Nammu was succeeded as ruler of Ur by Shulgi (2094–2046), who standardized not just the calendar but also the tax system and administration. He captured Susa, the capital of Elam (western Iran), which had long been a potent enemy of the Mesopotamian powers. Ur-Nammu created a major empire, stretching from modern Turkey to the Persian Gulf. However, under Shulgi's three successors, the territory receded. The Elamites invaded, sacked Ur in 2004, and made King Ibbi-Sin their captive.

The destruction of cities was a perpetual feature of Middle Eastern history. In some ways, the sack of Ur was the end of Sumer, which was quickly absorbed into Babylon. However, the Sumerian language remained, like Latin after the end of the Roman Empire.

The Elamites only lasted a couple of decades in Mesopotamia, though. There were other forces at play, both in Babylon to the south and in Ashur.

Chapter 3: The Old Assyrian Empire and Babylon

The first attested kings of Ashur emerged around 2025 BCE. These kings of the Old Assyrian period took advantage of the increasing precarity of Ur to set up their own kingdom. Ashur (the god) gave his name to the city, which, in turn, gave its name to the Assyrian people and the Assyrian nation (which included many people who were not ethnic Assyrians).

The Assyrian king lists include nearly thirty rulers who are otherwise unattested; nothing of them survives but their name. Among them is Ushpia, who is said to have built the temple of Ashur in the late 3rd millennium BCE. The king list includes "kings who lived in tents" and "kings who were ancestors," but it seems likely that they were added to the list later, possibly during Shamsi-Adad I's rule to incorporate his Amorite ancestors.

Ashur must have had governors under the rule of Ur, and it's likely that these governors simply claimed their independence after Ur fell to Elam and became kings. Possibly the first was Sulili, who might be the Ilaba-siululi mentioned as the governor of Ashur in a text from Ur. His seal is interesting, as it features the motto "Ashur is king." This shows a theocratic understanding of kingship, with the ruler acting as a steward for the god.

This was not a divine monarchy, like the pharaohs of ancient Egypt who were seen as incarnations of the god Horus (when alive) or Osiris (after death). Instead, it was a monarchy mandated by the god Ashur. In the early days of Ashur, the monarchy probably was a form of what we now call a constitutional monarchy, in which the hereditary leader ruled together with a popular assembly. These kings called themselves overseers, princes, or stewards.

The city assembly (*alum*) might have included all free adult men or consisted mainly of nobles.[i] Ot met near the Step Gate, by which a stele was erected detailing the city's laws, including commercial laws. The city hall (*bet alim*) was in charge of the treasury; it was not until later in Ashur's history that the king became the head of city hall (a position known as *limmum*). Years in Ashur were named after the *limmum*, not the king, unlike societies in the south of Mesopotamia.

The first line of kings that can be verified is the Puzur-Ashur dynasty or Old Assyrian dynasty. The style of kingship was perhaps not very different from what was going on in Babylon; however, the priesthood in Ashur was not nearly as strong as it was in Babylon. The king of Ashur (the city) effectively acted as the high priest of Ashur (the god).

Puzur-Ashur claimed Assyria's independence around 2025 BCE, though it is possible that he continued the lineage of earlier rulers. The succession was then unbroken from son to son for eight generations, with each becoming Ishiak Ashur, or vice-regent of Ashur. Under Puzur-Ashur's son Shalim-ahum, Ashur's trading network greatly increased, and under Erishum I (Shalim-ahum's grandson), the *karum* system of trading enclaves in Anatolian towns began.

A tablet from Kanesh, one of these enclaves, contains the invocation, "Ashur is king! Erishum is Ashur's Steward! He who tells a lie in the Step Gate, the demon of the ruins will smash his head like a pot that breaks."[ii]

There were *karum* trading posts in Kanesh, Hattusha, and Ankuwa, among other cities, where Assyrian merchants traded textiles, tin, iron, copper, wool, grain, gold, and silver. These *karum* weren't ruled by Assyria; rather, Assyrian merchants enjoyed special rights in each city and governed their own extra-territorial enclave. Local rulers had an incentive to set up a *karum* since they profited from the trade and

---

[i] Only about 50 percent of men were free; the rest were chattel slaves or debt slaves.

[ii] Frahm, Eckart. *Assyria: The Rise and Fall of the World's First Empire.* Basic Books, New York, 2023.

enjoyed privileged access to scarce goods.

Not all towns bought into the system, though. A letter found at Kanesh suggests traders on their way to the *karum* should hide tin in their underwear to avoid paying tolls on these goods at a less friendly town en route.[i]

Assyrians who traded and lived away from Ashur could take a wife in the place where they were living. Their wife in Ashur was considered the main wife, while the other was seen as a temporary arrangement. A secondary wife would likely see the marriage as beneficial. She would enjoy a good lifestyle while her husband was there, and when he went back to Ashur, she would get an amicable divorce, retaining the house and receiving a good payoff. She would also be able to remarry. This is an intriguing adaptation of the generally monogamous mores of Assyrians.

Women had a less privileged position in Assyrian society than they did in Sumer or Babylon. High-born women wore veils, and their contacts were highly controlled. Adultery was punished by death (though this was even-handed for both parties; there was no double standard). Women were dependent on their male relations.

During the latter part of the Puzur-Ashur dynasty, Assyria came under increasing pressure from the Amorites, who had already overrun the south of Mesopotamia. Erishum II was deposed, and the throne was taken by Shamshi-Adad I.

It is uncertain exactly who Shamshi-Adad was. He might have been an Amorite usurper, but the king list asserts that he was of the royal house of Ashur, descended from Ushpia. In that case, he might have been a cousin or another relation of the royal house who took power after Erishum proved unable to resist the Amorite threat. On the other hand, the mention of the house of Ushpia might be a later attempt to "legitimize" Shamshi-Adad and give the Assyrian monarchs a completely unbroken lineage from the earliest days. It is also possible that Shamshi-Adad was a member of the same extended family as Hammurabi, another expansionary ruler of the time.

Whichever is the case, Shamshi-Adad claimed the title of "king of the universe" and "unifier of the land between the two rivers." His rule was

---

[i] Frahm, Eckart. *Assyria: The Rise and Fall of the World's First Empire*. Basic Books, New York, 2023.

clearly expansionist. For instance, he took the city of Mari to the west. Ashur was the religious center of his realm. He rebuilt the god's temple in Ashur and added a ziggurat. He also appears to have been the first king to build a palace in Ashur. However, his capital was Shubat-Enlil in northeastern Syria, which was situated in a much more fertile region.

As the name of Shubat-Enlil ("Enlil's residence") suggests, the god to whom Shamshi-Adad gave particular worship was not Ashur but Enlil, the Sumerian storm god and creator. It must have been around this time that Enlil became identified with Ashur. While Ashur originally had been a single god with no family, this identification with Enlil gave him a wife, Enlil's wife Ninlil (Mullissu), and a son, Ninurta. The Assyrian pantheon was growing.

Shamshi-Adad reigned for thirty-three years, and one of the things we know about him is that he required a good stock of beer to be maintained for the palace. This was probably not just because he liked a drink or two. Beer was used in temple rituals. In fact, the entire brewing process was a ritual. The importance of ensuring that beer was correctly brewed can be seen by the fact that the Babylonian Code of Hammurabi required the death penalty for those guilty of watering down the beer they brewed or sold.

Brewing Assyrian Beer

This recipe is based on the Hymn to Ninkasi, a Sumerian text from around 1800 BCE that actually describes the brewing process as the goddess brews her beer.

On the first day, wheat grain is soaked in water. On the second day, the wheat is drained, put in a bowl, and covered. It is left until it begins to sprout. On the same day, bappir or beer bread is started. One would mix yeast, barley flour, and water and then set the mixture aside in a covered bowl for two days.

On the fourth day, the bappir is baked for ten minutes until just the crust is cooked, leaving the inside of the loaf raw. The wheat is also baked (nowadays, we would say "malted") in the same oven but for longer.

The next day, the wheat is crushed in a mortar, and the bappir is torn into pieces and placed in a pot with water. Dates and yeast are added to it (the Sumerians might have relied on wild yeasts). The pot is then covered and left to ferment for two days. In the high temperatures of Mesopotamia, fermentation would have occurred easily. Finally, the beer is filtered.

The Sumerians would have brewed on a large scale, but it's probably best if you just try for a couple of quarts. You'll need half a cup of wheat, a cup and a half of barley flour, half a cup of chopped dates, half a cup of honey, a couple of tablespoon of dried yeast, and two quarts of water.

This was a time when state formation was occurring in a number of different centers. Kanesh became an Anatolian power and eventually transformed into the center of the Hittite Empire, while Assyria began to expand beyond the Tigris to the Zagros Mountains.

Shamsi-Adad shared power with his two sons. Ishme-Dagan was made viceroy of Ekallatum, just north of Ashur, while Yasmah-Adad was given Mari. However, Yasmah-Adad was incompetent and often drunk, at least if his father's letters to him are to be believed. In one letter to Yasmah-Adad that was found at Mari, Shamsi-Adad compared Ishme-Dagan's military prowess with the way Yasmah-Adad lazed at ease with women. The message was clear: turn your life around!

Shamsi-Adad died in 1776 BCE at a time when Assyria was under attack. Yasmah-Adad had turned a deaf ear to his father's advice, as Mari was lost a few years after Shamsi-Adad's death. But Ishme-Dagan was made of sterner stuff. He created a joint enterprise with Dadusha, king of Eshnunna, which was located farther south. He was able to conquer the cities of Nineveh and Arbela with this support. Dadusha took the plunder, while Ishme-Dagan consolidated Nineveh into the Assyrian heartland. This was the first time that the core of the Assyrian Empire was united.

However, Ishme-Dagan's victories didn't last. Perhaps the king of Eshnunna realized that Ishme-Dagan had got the best out of the deal. Whatever the reason, Eshnunna turned into an implacable foe. Its people attacked Ishme-Dagan at Ashur and drove him into exile in Babylon.

The house of Shamsi-Adad failed after five monarchs. Puzur-Sin rose to power. This king portrayed himself as returning to the "true" line of Assyria, destroying the "evil" of his predecessors. However, by the time of Shalmaneser I in the Middle Assyrian Empire, Shamsi-Adad was thought of as a true Assyrian king and Puzur-Sin as the usurper.

At this point in the history of Mesopotamia, a new power arrived on the scene. The Amorites had migrated to Assyria and the south, bringing their Semitic language, Akkadian, with them. As well as taking over Ur and Lagash, an Amorite dynasty took over the previously unimportant city of Babylon. The first king of Babylon was Sumu-Abum, who reigned from around 1894 to 1881 BCE. He was followed by Sumu-la-El, who conquered the city of Kish.

The fifth king, Sin-Muballit, was the first to declare himself king of Babylon and expanded his territory by taking the cities of Isin, Borsippa, and Sippar. However, it was his son Hammurabi who built Babylon into a major power, as he took over most of southern Mesopotamia.

Hammurabi came to the throne around 1792 BCE while his father was still alive; Sin-Muballit had abdicated due to ill health. Hammurabi began his reign with a program of public works, including expansions to temples and improving the city walls. However, the Elamites' move into the plains, taking Eshnunna and other cities, forced Hammurabi to take a more active part in the region's military affairs. By allying himself with Larsa, he was able to send the Elamites packing.

However, relations with Larsa turned sour. Hammurabi took that city, Eshnunna, and other northern cities, including Mari. This gave him control of the entire southern part of Mesopotamia, bringing him up against Ashur in the north. (His destruction of the palace in Mari in 1759 BCE was a godsend to later archaeologists, as it left behind a huge number of easily dated, well-fired clay tablets. This archive included shopping lists, tax documents, legal cases, and personal letters.)

At first, Ishme-Dagan of Ashur allied with Hammurabi. Ashur was weak at the time, and Ishme-Dagan might have seen Babylon, a rising power, as a protector against the ever-threatening Elamites. However, this uneasy alliance did not hold, and eventually, Hammurabi took both Ashur and Nineveh. Ishme-Dagan I appears to have been forced to live in Babylon as a client king. His successor, Mut-Ashkur, was forced to pay tribute to Hammurabi.

The creation of this Babylonian superstate took Hammurabi twenty years, at the end of which he was truly entitled to call himself "king of Sumer and Akkad."

As king, Hammurabi had three tasks: to build, which he had done; to protect the state militarily, which he had done; and to preserve justice. The latter he did by issuing the Code of Hammurabi, known from the stele that is now in the Louvre in Paris, France. The top of the stele shows Hammurabi receiving the code from the god Shamash, and the inscription states the law was meant to protect the weak, orphans, and widows. In an empire where military might was often seen as right, the law offered recourse to those without power.

Law codes had been written before. For the first time, though, the law was written in Akkadian, not Sumerian. It covered a broad range of areas; for instance, it talked about the warranties on the sale of slaves, giving purchasers a form of consumer protection. It specified wage rates for craftsmen and seasonal laborers and rates of hire for boats. The code covered family law, inheritance, property title, and legal process. Rules for indemnities in the case of trespassing cattle were set (this was evidently a frequent problem), and merchants were indemnified if trading agents lost their cash. Reading the law code gives a good idea of how society was structured and how developed the Babylonian economy had become.

The stele on which Hammurabi's Code is written.[7]

The 3rd millennium BCE was a period of experimentation, with power shifting from city to city. But Shamsi-Adad and Hammurabi created a new idea, the idea of the territorial city, moving from the city-state to a state that included a number of cities. At the same time, the original idea of a hereditary civic leader ruling with a council was replaced by a monarchical ideal—the king who ruled in glorious isolation as the military leader and law-maker. That idea would prove to be very influential.

Hammurabi believed he had brought peace to Mesopotamia. He died around 1750 BCE, still believing that. However, peace did not survive for long after the accession of his son, Samsu-iluna. The kingdom of Sumer and Akkad began to fall apart. Puzur-Sin reclaimed Ashur, and in the south, the Sealand dynasty broke free, looking back to Sumerian times by using pseudo-Sumerian king names even though they spoke Akkadian.

Even so, from Hammurabi's reign onward, Assyria was highly influenced by trends and events in Babylon. Babylonia and Assyria were two separate, though related, empires, but it can sometimes be difficult to disentangle their two histories.

Middle Eastern Chronologies

Because there are few definite sources for dates in the earlier part of Mesopotamian history, historians have to base their datings on relative chronology. Dendrochronology, radiocarbon dating, and astronomical records have failed to fix dates closely enough to be certain.

A key source for chronology is the Venus Tablet of Ammisaduqa. This cuneiform text dates from the mid-17th century BCE and gives the time that Venus rises and sets on lunar dates for over twenty-one years. However, because Venus's visibility varies on an eight-year cycle, the start of the observations noted in the tablet could have taken place in 1702, 1646, 1638, 1582, or 1550 BCE. Dating systems based on these dates are referred to as the Long, Middle, Middle Low, Short, and Ultra Short chronologies.

For later periods, comparisons with the dates of Egyptian pharaohs and lunar observation dates can be used to give absolute dating. For instance, Ramesses II came to the throne in 1279 BCE, giving us a firm date to work with.

In 1595 BCE, Babylon was ruled by Hammurabi's great-great-grandson, Samsu-Ditana. The kingdom had shrunk, but it still was quite large, even including the city of Mari. Sealand continually threatened the Babylonians from the south, though.

However, events far to the north, in the Hittite capital of Hattusha (near modern Ankara), were responsible for Babylon's end. Mursili I conquered Aleppo in Syria, a prize that had eluded his predecessor. He decided Babylon, which was more than five hundred miles south, would be his next target. Mursili made his way down the Euphrates, plundering cities as he went. Goods and captives were sent back to Hattusha, leading to widespread depopulation. Perhaps realizing that it would be difficult to hold together a state that extended so far south, Mursili decided not to stay, instead simply taking his loot back with him. But it was too late for Babylon. He had put an end to Samsu-Ditana's rule, and Babylon was abandoned for some years.

(As a side note, Mursili might have made a mistake in returning to Hattusha, as he was assassinated soon after his return due to the Hittite royal family's infighting.)

It wasn't until 1530 BCE that Burnaburiash I, a Kassite, was able to take over Babylon and kickstart the city again. His son, Ulamburiash, conquered Sealand, putting Babylon back in control of the south. Around this time, Babylon adopted Marduk as its patron god, a decision that was crucial to later Babylonian religion and ideology. The new Kassite dynasty ruled Babylon for the next five hundred years.

Most of the historical sources from this period are commercial and private in nature. At the trading station in Kanesh, a huge number of dockets, bills, IOUs, and letters from one merchant to another have been found. The house of the merchant Usur-sha-Ishtar yielded more than two thousand separate documents. On the other hand, for the early kings of Assyria, there are very limited sources, which is a sharp contrast to the Neo-Assyrian Empire, where a very high proportion of extant documents come from royal holdings and are focused on the king.

Chapter 4: Restoration and Fall to the Mitanni

Babylon had been destroyed, and Ashur had fallen. Assyria entered a dark age for several centuries. While a king list exists for the period, there is little historical evidence about what happened in Assyria.

During this period, Assyria continued to change, moving ever further away from the status of a city-state. It became more of a larger entity governed by hereditary rulers. However, following the details of this change is extraordinarily difficult, owing to the lack of inscriptions and even archaeological data. One result of this black hole in data is that the book will have to fast-forward a couple of centuries.

Following Ishme-Dagan and Mut-Ashkur, who is not included in some versions of the king list, there appeared to have been fairly short reigns of eight different kings, lasting from 1765 to 1745. However, it is also possible that some of the names might be those of *limmum* who gave their names to the years of another king's reign. The last of these kings was Adasi, whose son, Bel-bani, succeeded him as king, founding the Adaside dynasty.

It is possible that the people of Assyria did not see this as a dark age. It is also possible that the lack of information is simply due to the fact that archaeologists have not excavated a source of documentation for this period that can deliver enough information. However, historians tend to think it was a dark age because Assyria was not involved in the events happening in the Middle East during this period. Events to the west and north of Ashur would have the biggest impact on Mesopotamia during the next few centuries.

For once, there were the Hittites to be reckoned with. Mursili had bypassed Ashur on his way to Babylon, but the Hittites had already destroyed Assyria's trading system. Hittite King Zuzzu destroyed Kanesh around 1710 BCE, and the rest of the system did not survive for long. And while the success of the Hittites did not last, it galvanized another people group, the Hurrians, to create their own state.

There were a number of small Hurrian principalities clustered in northwestern Syria and farther east in the mountains at the headwaters of the Tigris and Euphrates. These states started to coalesce into what would become Mitanni (Hanigalbat in Assyrian). Mitanni was established around 1600 BCE and became increasingly powerful in Mesopotamia.

At the same time, Egypt became an expansionary power and, for the first time, was looking beyond the Nile Valley. This brought Egypt and Mitanni into contact with each other, and they appeared to have enjoyed excellent diplomatic relations, even forming a pact against the Hittites.

Thutmose I became pharaoh around 1506, and early in his reign, he made an expedition to the north into Syria. He made his way as far as the Euphrates, setting up a stele on the banks of the river. (The Euphrates confused the Egyptians, who, living on the Nile, had never seen a river that flowed from north to south. They called the Euphrates the "backwards river.") However, this was purely a short-term punitive mission, as Thutmose did not expand the Egyptian kingdom into the Levant on a permanent basis.

Later, during the Eighteenth Dynasty of Egypt, Thutmose III, the grandson of Thutmose I (r. 1479–1425 BCE), led another campaign into Syria and then copied his grandfather's example by heading south to reach the Euphrates. Like Thutmose I, he erected a stele there. His main targets were a resurgent Hittite Empire and the Mitanni, both of which he pillaged extensively.

Thutmose III changed the balance of power. Egypt was now a force in the Middle East, not just in the Nile Valley, and Thutmose III received tribute from Assyria and Babylon, as well as from the Hittites. The Assyrian king who paid him tribute is not named in Thutmose's otherwise prolific inscriptions, but it was probably Ashur-nadin-ahhe I. Inevitably, the presence of both Mitanni and Egypt put pressure on Assyria, whose northern borders were at risk.

Few of these historical events appear in the Assyrian record. Assyria seems to have been something of a backwater, though the Adaside dynasty continued to rule and build. Between 1563 and 1548, for instance, Shamshi-Adad III rebuilt the temples and the city wall in Ashur. His successor, Ashur-nirari I, built a new palace in Ashur, and his son, Puzur-Ashur III, increased the city's size, adding a large suburb to the south. Puzur-Ashur is also said to have made a treaty with King Burnaburiash of Babylon, though the only evidence for this comes from a much later date.

However, the threat from Mitanni continued, and in 1465, the city of Ashur was sacked. The king of Mitanni, Shaushtatar, carried away a silver and gold door from the citadel, which was taken back to Ashur many years later, as well as other plunder and captives. Fortunately for Ashur, like the Hittites, the Mitanni had no desire to make Assyria a permanent part of their territory. When the Mitanni started to falter, Assyria was ready to pick up the pieces, creating the Middle Assyrian Empire, the subject of our next chapter.

Chapter 5: The Middle Assyrian Empire

Ashur-uballit I took power in Assyria just as the Mitanni was losing influence. The Mitanni were engaged in a civil war. Tushratta, the king of Mitanni, and a rival, Artatama, were fighting for control. Tushratta was eventually assassinated, and the Mitanni Empire was unstable for some time afterward, giving Ashur-uballit his chance to reestablish Assyria as a major power. It appears that Ashur-uballit's father, Eriba-Adad, might have made use of this instability by playing off different sides to create a pro-Assyrian faction in Mitanni. Ashur-uballit went a step further, defeating the Mitanni and securing tribute from its king.

Ashur-uballit ("Ashur-has-kept-alive") also expanded Assyria to the south. By the end of his reign, Assyria ruled Nineveh and probably also Arbela. These states were agriculturally richer than Ashur, and communication via the Tigris River were easier. Ashur-uballit also destroyed the Hurrian city of Arrapha (probably modern Kirkuk in northeastern Iraq) and divided its territories with Babylon.

Ashur-uballit was the first Assyrian ruler to use the title of king. Previously, rulers asserted that "Ashur is king and I am the representative of Ashur." Ashur-uballit I, on the other hand, used the title shar mat Ashur, "king of Ashur," instead of issi'ak Ashur, "governor of Ashur." Clearly, there had been a change in expectations of what a king was. There had also been a change in the vision of what Assyria ought to be. It was no longer seen as a small state based on a single city;

rather, it was seen as a major power.

Ashur-uballit corresponded with Pharaoh Akhenaten. This correspondence survived in Akhenaten's capital, along with other diplomatic correspondence written in Akkadian, which was the diplomatic language of the time. Early in his reign, Ashur-uballit sent a lump of lapis lazuli, a chariot, and two horses with his first letter. He sent two chariots, more lapis lazuli, and a request for twenty talents of gold with his second letter. He was building a new palace, he said, and wanted Akhenaten to send enough gold to decorate it. Neither letter seems to have been written with great elegance or much tact.

What's particularly interesting is that Ashur-uballit signed his letter as not just "king" but "great king." In doing so, he was putting himself on the same level as the big players—Egypt, Babylon, the Hittites, and the Mitanni.

Ashur-uballit also maintained good relations with Babylon. With the Mitanni still potentially a threat on the northern borders, it made sense to have diplomatic ties to the south. He married his daughter, Muballitat-Sherua, to Burnaburiash II of Babylon. Their son Karahardash became king of Babylon. Evidently, Ashur-uballit's objective was to bring the two states of Ashur and Babylon into the same family and perhaps even under the same rule.

However, things did not work out quite as he had planned. Events took an unexpected turn. Karahardash was executed by an anti-Assyrian faction, which replaced him on the throne by the non-royal Nazibugash. Those Babylonians who didn't want an Assyrian on the throne would be disappointed, though. Karahardash's fate gave Ashur-uballit the excuse he needed to invade Babylon. He defeated the usurper and installed another of his grandsons, Kurigalzu II, on the Babylonian throne.

This worked for a while. But Kurigalzu, who had been brought up in Babylon even if his mother was an Assyrian princess, seemed to have eventually come to resent the Assyrian influence in his kingdom and invaded Assyria. A battle took place at Sugagu, which is only a day's journey south of Ashur. There are two accounts of this battle. One reports a Babylonian victory, while the other says Assyria, under Ashur-uballit's son Enlil-nirari won the day.

Whatever happened at Sugagu, Assyria was headed toward creating an empire. Ashur had become the capital of an expansionary state that relied on its military might to increase its territories. "Assyrian" now meant being a subject of the empire, not a person from the city of Ashur. Popular representation in the city council appeared to have ended, and the monarchy became the sole authority in Assyria.

The rise of kingly power necessitated the creation of an Assyrian court, which included eunuchs (who were barred from becoming kings, making them "safe" servants and ministers) and a harem.[1] Bureaucratic documents ceased to be the affairs of the city and instead became the affairs of the king.

Archaeologist Bleda Düring sees the Middle Assyrian Empire as the first lasting empire of the age. Earlier imperial states had managed to last for no more than a century, and most of them were short-lived empires based on conquests that fell apart once the founder's impetus had disappeared. Assyria survived the Bronze Age collapse, and its empire lasted for seven hundred years. This, Düring emphasizes, was a major achievement that has rarely been matched in history.

Although Assyria defeated the Babylonians, there was a good deal of Babylonian influence in Assyria at this time, particularly in regards to religion. Many of the Babylonian gods appeared in Assyrian religion. They were sometimes given new names. The city of Babylon's god, Marduk, was now worshiped in Ashur.

Ashur-uballit's great-grandson Adad-nirari I (r. 1305–1274) and his son Shalmaneser I (r. 1273–1244) continued the expansion of Assyria. Adad-nirari called himself "pacifier of all enemies above and below," fighting the Kassite dynasty of Babylon to the south and the Mitanni and Hittites to the north. (By this point, the Mitanni had been reduced to a vassal state of the Hittite Empire.)

Adad-nirari fought his way along the Khabur River in northeastern Syria, a region that was both fertile and densely populated. He made the king of Mitanni pay him tribute. When payments stopped coming, he sacked the capital, Washukanni, and kidnapped the royal family. After this, he started calling himself "king of the universe" (the same title used by Shamshi-Adad I), putting other kingdoms on notice that his ambitions

---

[1] A harem from a later period was found in the palace at Nimrud and was excavated from 1988 into the 1990s. Because of subsequent wars in Iraq, the discovery has not been properly assessed or published. Intriguingly, archaeologist Muzahim Mahmoud Hussein found four tombs of royal wives under the floors of the harem; the women of the harem lived with their predecessors buried directly underfoot.

were limitless.

However, it was Adad-nirari's successor, Shalmaneser I, who ended the Mitanni Empire for good. Despite the Hittites' assistance, Shattuara II of Mitanni could not stand against the might of Assyria. Shalmaneser integrated the new territory into Assyria by appointing his younger brother, Ibashshi-ili, as chancellor of Assyria in the newly built city of Dur-Katlimmu. The chancellor was given the title "king of Hanigalbat" ("king of Mitanni"), but it was only a courtesy title; he was clearly responsible to Shalmaneser. A temple was built at Dur-Katlimmu to the god associated with the royal family, Salmanu. (Shalmaneser means "Salmanu is eminent.")

Shalmaneser was probably the first king to use wholesale deportations as a means of building his empire. From this time onward, it became a regular method of Assyrian imperialism. Deporting people allowed Assyria to take possession of craftsmen or professional laborers by bringing them to the capital or sending them to cities that needed assistance. For instance, farmers might be reassigned to an area where fertility was low to improve agricultural methods. (The experience of Ashur's traders, who often lived in Kanesh and other cities for years on end, might have made this feel quite normal to the Assyrians, though it doesn't to us.)

Additionally, reassigning populations to new areas would help create "Assyrians" by reducing feelings of local identities. It also deprived conquered areas of potential leaders who might rebel against Assyrian rule.

Throughout the history of Assyria, there are a few "sweet spots" where three or four great rulers appeared in a row. Tukulti-Ninurta I was the successor to Shalmaneser. He came to the throne in 1244 BCE and reigned for around thirty-seven years, during which he both consolidated the northwest of Assyria and reasserted Assyrian rule over Babylon.

Tukulti-Ninurta I justified the invasion by asserting that the Babylonian king, Kashtiliash IV, had broken his agreements with Assyria. Kashtiliash was captured. Tukulti-Ninurta ritually trod on Kashtiliash's neck, using him as a footstool, and brought him to Ashur. He then installed a series of puppet rulers in Babylon. The first two proved useless and were rapidly replaced. Tukulti-Ninurta called himself ruler of "Sumer and Akkad" as the Babylonian kings had before him; by that point, it was an archaism, but it enshrined his claim to power over southern Mesopotamia as well as Assyria. The third puppet ruler, Adad-shuma-iddina, lasted six years before Tukulti-Ninurta deposed him, sacking Babylon and taking the statue of Marduk, Babylon's god, to Ashur. Tukulti-Ninurta called himself ruler of Sumer and Akkad as the Babylonian kings had before him; by then, it was an archaic title, but it enshrined his claim to power over southern Mesopotamia as well as Assyria.

Tukulti-Ninurta brought a huge number of texts from Babylon. These included works on divination, medical texts, prayers and liturgies, literary works, lists of gods, and Sumerian word lists. Scribes in Assyria could use old Babylonian cuneiform and the even older Sumerian language for their own writing.

Assyrian kings were expected to be builders and warriors, and Tukulti-Ninurta did not disappoint. He built a new temple to Ishtar in Ashur and also created a new trade town, Kar-Tukulti-Ninurta, which was just upstream on the Tigris from Ashur. This town had a new palace, a temple to Ashur, and a ziggurat.

Pride always comes before a fall. No temple to Ashur had ever been erected outside the god's own city, and the creation of Kar-Tukulti-Ninurta might have been unpopular with the people in Ashur. Worse, Babylon turned against Tukulti-Ninurta again later in his reign. This time, the Babylonian revolt, led by Adad-shuma-usur (possibly a son of the deposed Kashtiliash), was successful. The Assyrian army had become overextended and was struggling to hold on to all the territories that had been gained since Adad-nirari I's accession.

Tukulti-Ninurta was becoming increasingly unpopular at home since his string of military successes had come to an end. His move to the new city, together with his plundering of temples in Babylon, were seen as tempting the gods to punish Assyria. In 1207 BCE, a coup d'etat took place. Tukulti-Ninurta was assassinated by his sons. Assyria's fortunes were no longer headed upward; the wheel of fortune had turned.

Chapter 6: Assyria during the Bronze Age Collapse

While Assyria was focused on its rivalry with Babylon, the world around it had been changing dramatically. First, around 1200 BCE, the Sea Peoples arrived, attacking the coasts of the eastern Mediterranean. Their origins remain a mystery, but they clearly posed a formidable threat to settled civilizations in the Levant and Egypt.

In 1177, Pharaoh Ramesses III was able to defeat them on the Egyptian coast. However, Egypt was greatly weakened by the need to fight them off and eventually lost its eastern colonies. Nevertheless, Egypt survived. Other states were not so lucky. Mycenaean Greece was almost completely destroyed. Greece saw its population decline, with people migrating to Cyprus and the Levant. However, Athens survived to take its place later in history.

The Hittite state had already been damaged by Tukulti-Ninurta's attacks. The Sea Peoples put further pressure on the Hittites, taking Cilicia, Cyprus, and most of Canaan. This cut off the Hittites from their trade routes and left them vulnerable to attacks both from the Mediterranean and from Assyria to the south. A few Hittite city-states survived, such as Carchemish and Melid, but Assyria made them tributary states and later incorporated them fully into the Neo-Assyrian Empire.

Babylon's Kassite dynasty fell in 1155 after being conquered by Elam. In fact, Elam had overrun most of Babylonia by 1158 BCE. Assyria was able to take a good deal of Babylonian territory when the last Kassite king of Babylon, Enlil-nadin-ahi, was defeated and taken captive. The next dynasty was based in the city of Isin before Itti-Marduk-balatu managed to retake Babylon in the 1130s.

In the Levant, a number of states fell. Ugarit, an important port on the Syrian coast with trade links to Egypt, was destroyed around 1200 BCE; it was never rebuilt. Other Amorite states, such as Qatna and Alalakh, had already been abandoned by 1300, and the survivors, such as Amurru, collapsed or were destroyed during the Bronze Age collapse. There was a decline in trade in the eastern Mediterranean since most economies were stagnating.

Egypt suffered too despite Ramesses's victory over the Sea Peoples. Egypt slowly declined until 1078 when the New Kingdom came to an end with the death of Ramesses XI and the Third Intermediate Period started, during which the country was divided between the rule of Tanis in the Nile Delta and Thebes, which ruled Middle and Upper Egypt.

There are numerous theories as to why the Bronze Age collapse happened; it was probably a combination of causes. Climate change caused some of the migrations, which put pressure on established states once those new people arrived. The Hekla 3 eruption in Iceland might have led to widespread air pollution, disrupting agriculture. In the Near East, there were a number of droughts; in some areas, yields fell to such an extent that the land ceased to be cultivated.

The beginning of ironmaking also created technological turbulence, which must have changed the competitive nature among states. Egypt, for instance, was very late to adopt ironworking and relied on external supplies of the metal, putting it at a disadvantage despite its impressive military power.

Politically, the Bronze Age collapse virtually wiped out the "palace states." New groups were less hierarchical and often based on ethnicity, such as the Philistines, Arabs, and Aramaeans. The Bronze Age collapse also wiped out the use of cuneiform script in the Mediterranean. From this point onward, alphabetic scripts began to be used in the Levant. Cuneiform was restricted to use in Mesopotamia and Persia.

The Bronze Age collapse appears to have started in the Mediterranean Basin, so it took time for the effects to be seen in Mesopotamia. Initially, Assyria seemed to have benefited from the distress of many of its westerly rivals.

Tiglath-Pileser I (r. 1114-1076) was one of Assyria's greatest kings. He made Assyria the leading power of the Middle East, which it remained so for the next five hundred years. He led an expedition into Anatolia, Cappadocia, and Syria, expanding Assyrian dominions far to the north and west and as far as the Mediterranean. He took tribute from the cities of Sidon and Byblos in modern Lebanon.

However, these victories were difficult to consolidate. The mountainous territory, which was very different from the Mesopotamian plains, allowed Assyria's enemies to operate a guerrilla resistance and prevent Assyria from setting up a lasting administration in these areas. Perhaps as a result of these difficulties, Tiglath-Pileser started the custom of taking royal princes as hostages, ensuring their fathers' obedience. The princes would be educated as Assyrian princes, giving them a strong sense of Assyrian culture and ideology. The idea was to eventually make them into vassal kings.

Tiglath-Pileser also planted foreign trees in Ashur. Mesopotamia had few trees of its own, so the Assyrians were fascinated by the trees they saw elsewhere. Although what remains of the Assyrian kings is their buildings, they also created huge gardens.

Tiglath-Pileser's conquests did not last. By the time of Ashurnasirpal I (r. 1049-1031), Assyria had shrunk back to its heartlands and was under attack by Aramaean raiders. After his reign, there are no records of any military campaigns led by Assyria for almost a century. Under his younger son and third successor, Ashur-Rabi II (r. 1012-972), Assyria even managed to lose its cities on the Euphrates.

However, Ashur itself was never conquered, and power remained in the hands of the Adaside dynasty. This would give Assyria an important advantage when things began to change.

Chapter 7: The Neo-Assyrian Empire

If the Bronze Age collapse was at least partly caused by climatic change, so, too, was the rebirth of the empire. However, in this case, it was not because of widespread drought. Increasing rainfall improved agricultural productivity in Mesopotamia, kickstarting local economies and creating new agricultural surpluses that could be invested in building, improving irrigation, or (the Assyrians' choice) creating an army for taking over neighboring states.

The Aramaeans were no longer a potent threat. Many had settled in the Near East, and those who had moved into Assyria had become naturalized. Large-scale migration, which had been part of the Bronze Age collapse, was no longer occurring, so fighting off incursions was no longer the top need.

This gave Assyria a huge opportunity, and its rulers seized it with both hands. Assyria came out of the starting block fast, taking advantage of its rivals' weaknesses. Assyrian rulers had a single objective: to restore Assyria to its greatest extent. Many of the kings of this period were named after earlier great rulers, harkening back to the Middle Assyrian period as the "classical" age of Assyrian culture and aiming to emulate their achievements.

Late in the Neo-Assyrian Empire, King Esarhaddon wrote, "Before me, cities; behind me, ruins," a phrase that encapsulates the hunger and aggression of Assyrian rulers during this period.[i]

However, this was no longer an empire based on opportunistic military adventures. Innovations in government administration, together with the new ideology of absolute kingship, made it the first of the great world empires. Egypt, which was shut away in the Nile Valley anyway, was slightly apart from the rest of the world, so it was behind technologically, putting it out of competition. Greece was still in the early stages of its development. It was divided into a mass of small city-states in much the way Mesopotamia had been during early Sumerian times.

Ashur-Dan II (r. 934–912 BCE) is usually considered the first ruler of the Neo-Assyrian Empire since he reconquered much of Assyria's lost territory. In particular, he aimed at ensuring the trade routes into Anatolia were free from danger and retook land to the west that had come under Aramaean rule.

Assyrian warfare could be brutal. When Ashur-Dan II took Kadmuhu in the northwest, he executed the ruler and had his flayed skin displayed on the walls of Arbela. However, Ashur-Dan also resettled indigent Assyrians in fertile areas and started a program of land reclamation.

His son, Adad-nirari II (r. 911–891 BCE), expanded the empire further, though he appears to have had to fight off some opportunistic rebellions when he succeeded his father. In particular, he turned his sights south, twice defeating Babylon and pushing Assyrian rule downriver. He also created vassal states in the Khabur area in Syria.

However, he was able to use diplomacy wisely, concluding an advantageous peace treaty with Babylon. He and the king of Babylon, Nabu-shuma-ukin, married each other's daughters. (Though the Babylonian Chronicles are fragmentary, it might have been the next Assyrian ruler, Tukulti-Ninurta II, who swapped daughters.)

With Adad-nirari II, Assyrian history arrives at a very important point. From the first year of his reign, 911 BCE, there is a full record for every year of every Assyrian ruler, which allows for more precise dating of events from this time onward.

---

[i] Frahm, Eckart. *Assyria: The Rise and Fall of the World's First Empire.* Basic Books, New York, 2023.

Tukulti-Ninurta II (r. 890–884 BCE) took the name of an illustrious predecessor like his father and grandfather. He campaigned along both the Euphrates and the Upper Tigris, consolidating his father's gains. He took tribute, including horses for his army. The amount of tribute taken each time might have been small, but everything was added to the central treasury, which enabled a prolific building program at Ashur and Nineveh.

One of Tukulti-Ninurta's inscriptions sums up the priorities of his reign: "to her lands I added land, and to her people, I added people."

Ashurnasirpal II succeeded his father in 883 BCE. Four years later, he made a momentous decision and moved the capital of the Assyrian state from Ashur to Kalhu (today known as Nimrud). Until that point, Kalhu had been a small provincial capital. Ashurnasirpal also undertook an extensive rebuilding program in Ashur and continued to use the vaults under Ashur's Old Palace as the mausoleum of the Assyrian monarchs. He clearly knew the story of Tukulti-Ninurta I's fated move of the capital to Kar-Tukulti-Ninurta and his assassination by his sons. He was determined to keep the priesthood and nobles in Ashur on his side.

He also kept on the good side of Tukulti-Ninurta's master scholar, Gabbu-ilani-eresh. This was a more important post than it sounds; it would be equivalent to a chief of staff or head of strategy today. A number of later master scholars (ummanu or tupshar sharri, "king's scribe") traced their descent to Gabbu-ilani-eresh, so it seems that the post was hereditary.

Kalhu was a good choice since it was a central region in Assyria; Ashur was peripheral, located to the south and west of the center of the state. Kalhu also had space to expand, while Ashur was limited by the curve of the river on which it was built.

A lamassu guards the gate of Ashurnasirpal's palace in Kalhu.[a]

The move also gave Ashurnasirpal the chance to refresh his administration. He kept the master scholar but handpicked the other officials he wanted to take with him. This weakened the power of the nobility, who were left behind in the now peripheral cities of Ashur, Nineveh, and Arbela. Ashurnasirpal brought more eunuchs into his bureaucracy. They could not aspire to be king since a king had to be perfect in body. Reliefs show more and more clean-shaven men; almost all of these men would have been eunuchs.

Ashurnasirpal changed the balance of power within Assyria in favor of the king and to the detriment of high-ranking families and temple priesthoods. He also changed the nature of the Assyrian state. Unlike earlier rulers of the Neo-Assyrian Empire, he assimilated his conquests into the Assyrian kingdom rather than leaving them as vassal states. Assyria moved from needing tribute to rebuild its cities and armies to having enough resources to invest in administering new territories.

Kalhu (Nimrud) was created at least partly by craftsmen who had been resettled from elsewhere in the empire. It had nine temples and a north-west palace. The palace marked a major departure from city-planning norms since it dominated the entire city. At Ashur and elsewhere, the building that dominated the skyline had always been the city god's temple or ziggurat; now, the kingship was asserting itself much more strongly.

The palace was a masterpiece. It was also an ideological assertion of Ashurnasirpal's control of his universe. Human-headed winged bulls (*lamassu*) up to sixteen feet high guarded the gates as protection, and alabaster reliefs celebrated the king's achievements. One scene shows Ashurnasirpal raising his hand in worship to a god in a winged sun disk. A protective spirit stands behind the king, guarding him. In the center is the "sacred tree" motif, a symbol of fertility and prosperity. Clearly, Ashurnasirpal's reign was mandated by the gods, according to this and other similar scenes. These scenes were copied again and again, not just in the palace but also on royal seals.

Ashurnasirpal raises his hand toward the symbol of Ashur.⁹

The palace had three courtyards: one for state business, one for the administration, and one for the royal family. Each room had glazed brick or painted walls above the stone reliefs and a ceiling made of Lebanese cedar beams. The themes of the reliefs are varied. They included military campaigns, hunting parties, rituals, and protective deities. Ashurnasirpal's palace was probably the first use of such extensive reliefs in Assyrian history; they became a precedent for every later Assyrian ruler's building works.

Ashurnasirpal channeled the Zab River to irrigate pleasure gardens full of exotic plants. These gardens might have been the ancestors of the much later Persian and Mughal *charbagh*, which was known for its lush vegetation and central water channels.

Ashurnasirpal's Banquet Stele gives the menu he served his guests at a huge ten-day "palace-warming" feast: one thousand oxen, one thousand calves, ten thousand sheep, fifteen thousand lambs, five hundred stags, five hundred gazelles, one thousand ducks, five hundred geese, ten thousand doves, ten thousand fish, and ten thousand loaves of bread. This was all washed down with ten thousand jars of beer. Snacks included nuts, salted seeds, pistachios, and olives.

Ashurnasirpal was not prone to understatement. An inscription at the temple of Ninurta claims, "I am king, I am lord, I am praiseworthy, I am exalted, I am important, I am magnificent, I am foremost, I am a hero, I am a warrior, I am a lion, and I am a man."[1]

Several other things changed besides the idea of the monarchy. For instance, while the Code of Hammurabi was still known, it was used as a statement of ideal justice rather than as a practical legal text. There was no separate judiciary. Either state officials or temple personnel adjudicated; the king generally only became involved in cases of treason. The king might also be called in if people stole from temples. Since the gods were responsible for protecting the king and the state, theft from temples jeopardized the empire and was taken extremely seriously.

Messenger services were being developed, along with royal roads. This helped the empire to improve, as it increased the distance over which direct government was effective.

Though beer remained the staple drink in Mesopotamia, as more wine-producing territories entered the empire, drinking imported wine became an affordable luxury for the wealthier Assyrians. Some of those Assyrians probably became even wealthier by importing it!

Although it was Ashurnasirpal II who moved the court to Kalhu, it was his son, Shalmaneser III, who built it into a major imperial center. By this point, Assyria was the major power in the region. It was much larger than any of the states around it. The old settlement mound at Kalhu became the citadel, and the rest of the city was surrounded by a four-mile-long wall, with a second citadel in a corner to provide further protection. This became the pattern for later capitals, including Nineveh and Dur-Sharrukin (present-day Khorsabad). There was no temple for Ashur, who remained only the god of his own city. Ishtar and other deities had temples at Kalhu, though.

Kalhu was excavated by Max Mallowan from 1949 to 1957. He found a huge number of documents in the palace, including letters that throw light on Assyrian campaigns against Babylon, as well as royal building projects. (Mallowan is an archaeologist who is not quite as well known as his wife, who also came on the dig at Nimrud. Who was she? Well, she

---

[1] Frahm, Eckart. *Assyria: The Rise and Fall of the World's First Empire.* Basic Books, New York, 2023.

was the famous murder mystery writer Agatha Christie.)

Ashurnasirpal had fully restored the borders of the empire; Shalmaneser wanted to go further. He led more than thirty military campaigns during his thirty-five-year reign. Heading west, he took Bit-Adini and renamed its capital Kar-Shulmanu-ashared, "Shalmaneser's trading post." He then relocated native Assyrians to Kar- Shulmanu-ashared, probably to transfer Assyrian government and commercial norms, as well as to ensure the city's loyalty.

The borders of Assyria had previously ebbed and flowed with time since the army was based in the capital and could not always arrive in time to resist pressure from enemies or rebellious vassals. The army was also based on temporary levies, which meant raising an army took time.

Shalmaneser took action to make the empire bulletproof. He established a standing army and stationed units in the four border marches. The official in charge of each army was entrusted with great power, which could become a problem should any of them decide to rebel. However, the fact that they could act quickly and on their own initiative enabled Assyria to react rapidly to any outside threats. In many cases, eunuchs were chosen for the border march "field marshal" positions.

Shalmaneser also created a strong cavalry division. Chariots were good vehicles for the steppes and plains, but they were not useful in the mountains. Extending army operations outside Mesopotamia required a more flexible response. (Chariots had to be taken apart, carried through mountain passes, and then put together again before engaging the enemy. So, while they remained high-status vehicles, they were a strategic weakness.)

Shalmaneser raided far outside the borders of the empire. In the Levant, he created a number of client states, including Judah. He eventually occupied most of Syria and Arabia.[i]

However, one thing Shalmaneser did not do was invade Babylon. Instead, he made it a firm ally. When he led a campaign into Babylon, it was to save Marduk-zakir-shumi I, the rightful king, from a rebellion led by his younger brother. After two campaigns, Shalmaneser finally managed to run the rebel to ground and killed him. Shalmaneser's

---

[i] Ahab, King of Israel, together with Hadadezer of Damascus, fought against Shalmaneser at the Orontes River. Jehu later brought fought against Shalmaneser tribute.

throne dais shows the two kings grasping each other's hands in friendship.

In old age, Shalmaneser had to hand over the leadership of military campaigns to his commander in chief, Dayyan-Assur. This ordinarily would not be worthy of notice, but Shalmaneser's Black Obelisk mentioned Dayyan-Assur. This was the first time a royal inscription had ever ascribed a victory to anyone other than the king.

The end of Shalmaneser's reign saw a threat to the succession. Shalmaneser had made his younger son, Shamshi-Adad, crown prince, but his elder son, Ashur-dain-aplu, rebelled. This rebellion was eventually crushed, but in order to do so, Assyria had to rely on Babylonian help. Marduk-zakir-shumi was happy to return the favor Shalmaneser had done him, and Shamshi-Adad V inherited the throne in 824 BCE.

The succession struggle had weakened Assyria, and nobles who had seen Dayyan-Assur's magnificent conquests wanted a piece of the Assyrian pie for themselves. So, Shamshi-Adad started with a disadvantage. Several client kingdoms attempted to withhold tribute, spotting potential weakness. Shamshi-Adad appeared to have struggled for about a decade before finding his feet. He also appeared to have resented the fact that during the earlier part of his reign, Babylon held the upper hand.

So, despite his father's friendship with Marduk-zakir-shumi, Shalmaneser took his troops south and ended up getting a treaty with Marduk-zakir-shumi that was in his favor. Later, he campaigned twice against the succeeding king, Marduk-balassu-iqbi, who might have been his brother-in-law. After making his way to the east of the Tigris, Shalmaneser was able to avoid the Babylonian fort at Zaddi and head for the center of Babylonia. He boasted of taking more than thirty thousand captives during his second campaign. Shamshi-Adad later fought against the next Babylonian king, Baba-aha-iddina, taking him captive too.

Babylonia was in disarray. There is no record of a king in Babylon for at least a decade after Baba-aha-iddina. The empire was ripe for the picking. But when Shamsi-Adad died in 811, his successor, Adad-nirari III, was probably too young to exercise his rule effectively. His mother, Shammuramat, might have acted as regent. She was the only Assyrian queen to have retained her title after her husband's death, making her a rare feminine figure in what is an almost exclusively male narrative. She had a stele erected in her honor in Ashur (another exception to the men's club rules) and even accompanied Adad-nirari on a campaign.

Adad-nirari III was never a strong king. The eunuch Palil-eresh governed the western half of Assyria and appeared to have done so semi-independently. This might have worried Adad-nirari; a few years before his death, he installed a new general, Shamshi-ilu. Shamshi-ilu quickly consolidated his power over the army and over the western half of the empire. On one of his steles, Shamshi-ilu omitted the king's name and took all the credit himself. This was unprecedented.

During these four decades, Assyria was strong economically. It saw the increased production of good and an increase in the population that gave it a sturdy base; the empire simply had an internal focus, not an external one, and no strong leadership. Plagues occurred during this period, and consequent quarantines and lockdowns interfered with trade, but the underlying economy was strong.

Tiglath-Pileser III (r. 745–727) was able to launch a new expansion campaign. The circumstances under which he came to the throne are not clear, nor is his parentage; he might have been a son of his predecessor, Ashur-nirari V, or of Adad-nirari III (in which case he took the throne from his brother). It is possible he came to power as the result of a coup d'etat.

Tiglath-Pileser transformed Assyria into a true empire, doubling its size despite his relatively short reign of eighteen years. He centralized authority, bringing new men into the administration and cutting back the power of the nobles. He ensured that each noble's land holdings were widely dispersed across the empire so that no individual could accumulate a strong position in any single province.

A mural from Tiglath-Pileser III's palace in Til Barsip showing him giving an audience.[10]

Unlike Shamshi-Adad V, Tiglath-Pileser hit the ground running. He had no sooner acceded to the throne than he invaded north and eastern Babylon. In the same year, he took action to suppress restive Aramaean tribes near the Assyrian borders.

In 743, he defeated Urartu. In 740, he conquered Arpad and made northern Syria into a new province. Later, he consolidated his dominion over modern Lebanon and made Judah, Moab, and Edom into tributary states. He even reached the Egyptian border. By 734, he had annexed Damascus and had made Hoshea his puppet king in Israel.

By Tiglath-Pileser's time, chariots had become larger. Three men drove them rather than only two. The driver and the archer had a third man tasked with protecting them. The chariots were also heavier due to having more armor.

Tiglath-Pileser III in his chariot with the royal parasol held over him.[11]

Babylon was a prize that two Assyrian kings had left untouched. Tiglath-Pileser bided his time for more than a decade. But finally, he found conditions had moved in his favor. In 734, Babylonian King Nabonassar died. His son, Nabu-nadin-zeri, succeeded him, but he only lasted a little more than a year before he was killed by one of his provincial governors, Nabu-shuma-ukin. This usurper lasted just a month before a Chaldean (southern Babylonian), Nabu-mukin-zeri, put down the rebellion and took the throne himself. This left Babylon looking ripe for the picking, and Tiglath-Pileser took full advantage. In 729, he invaded Babylon and proclaimed himself king of Babylon.

Tiglath-Pileser united the two kingdoms under his personal rule. This was not a political union. Babylon remained a separate kingdom and was not brought into the Assyrian system of government.

Tiglath-Pileser's son, Shalmaneser V, continued the expansion and brought Israel's independence to an end by annexing Samaria. However, his reign was brief, lasting just five years, from 727 to 722 BCE.

He was succeeded by Sargon II (r. 722–705 BCE). Evidence is hard to find, but Sargon might have led a palace coup in 722 that put Shalmaneser out of power after just five years of rule. On the other hand, the Babylonian Chronicles simply say, "Shalmaneser died." Sargon's name was a reference to the Akkadian Empire and its greatest king; perhaps, ironically, the name Sargon, or Sharrukin in Assyrian, means "the legitimate king."

Sargon II was probably a younger son of Tiglath-Pileser, but he is generally regarded as the founder of a new dynasty. Babylonian inscriptions assign him to the dynasty of Hanigalbat rather than that of Baltil, the Assyrian main line. This suggests he might have been from a lateral branch of the family or perhaps was a son of the monarch's younger brother.

Sargon was a decisive leader, using both military action and spectacle to achieve his aims. He had a highly developed sense of *realpolitik* and how to get his way with both allies and enemies. Sargon had to put down a rebellion in Palestine almost immediately, but he also needed a strategy to hold back a resurgent Elamite kingdom. His solution was neatly calculated; he made peace with Elam and put down the rebellions by Ilu-bi'di and Hanunu, flaying one and blinding the other. Harsh punishment and clemency were weapons; he could play "good cop" or "bad cop" and often aimed to achieve a balance of the two to encourage others to do what he wanted.

His earlier conquests included Carchemish, which he conquered in 717. He looted the treasury, taking an immense amount of silver. In 714, he conquered Urartu and made a surprise attack on Musashir with a small raiding party after having made his way through very difficult mountain territory. Musashir was a rich city, and its contents were accounted for by Sargon II's scribes. The Assyrians took silver and gold from the temple, over twenty-five thousand bronze shields, and hundreds of thousands of bronze daggers.

Sargon increased the size of his army by taking charioteers (and presumably other forces) from conquered peoples. For instance, he acquired fifty chariot teams from Samaria, two hundred from Hamath, and fifty from Carchemish. A chariot was an expensive asset, so the owners of these teams were probably rich men or nobility. By taking them into his army, he killed two birds with one stone, turning these opinion-makers into loyal subjects and increasing his military resources.

The result of this recruitment can clearly be seen from the fact that a fifth of his army had non-Assyrian names. The army, as well as the empire, was becoming increasingly ethnically diverse.

In 710 BCE, he turned his attention to the reconquest of Babylonia. By now, Sargon had a seasoned army full of campaign veterans. Babylon, on the other hand, was divided between the urban population and semi-independent tribes in the marshes. The succession of a new king in Elam had put Babylon's ability to access help from the Elamites in question. Marduk-apla-Iddina II was tactically clever and avoided battles where he could, but Assyria was winning supporters among the governors and the tribes. Several cities defected to Sargon's side.

The Assyrian forces were getting ever closer to the capital, and when Elam explicitly stated that it would not help Babylon, Marduk-apla-iddina fled to the marshes in the south. Cleverly, Sargon consolidated his control of the north of Babylon before heading south for a final confrontation with Marduk-apla-Iddina, who was hiding out in his home city, Dur-Yakin. Marduk-apla-iddina flooded the fields around Dur-Yakin, breaking down all the bridges and causeways to impede Sargon's approach. Marduk-apla-iddina was partly successful, as the city managed to withstand Sargon's blockade for a year before finally negotiating a treaty. Marduk-apla-Iddina was exiled to Elam—an example of Sargon's occasional and usually well-judged clemency.

The priests of Babylon, who appeared to have been more powerful than the priests of Ashur, took matters into their own hands and invited Sargon into the city and then into the temple to grasp Marduk's hand at the New Year festival, making him king. He stayed in Babylon until 707.

When Sargon II returned to Assyria, he moved the capital to Dur-Sharrukin, "Sargon's Fort" (modern-day Khorsabad). It took him ten years to build. Moving the capital might not have been a simple whim; by creating a new capital, Sargon was expanding the economy, opening new land to cultivation, and improving living standards. The new capital fulfilled the same objectives as a modern urban gentrification project. It was a massive construction program. Craftsmen and laborers who came to work on it had their debts forgiven. (It is worth noting that those whose land was acquired for the project were given monetary compensation. The king was not above the law. Some were offered land in other parts of Assyria.)

Around Dur-Sharrukin, olive groves were planted. Olive oil was a scarce resource in Assyria, so this was a practical and potentially profitable move.

Dur-Sharrukin was splendid. It had a citadel with a 165-foot-high ziggurat, a royal palace, and numerous temples. The palace covered twenty-five acres, and its gates were guarded by colossal winged bulls. Its walls were 16,280 Assyrian units in length. That number was important; the Assyrians were great believers in numerology, and 16,280, translated into letters, added up to the name "Sargon." These walls had 157 towers. Temples to Adad, Ningal, Ninurta, Nabu, Shamash, and Sin were erected, and a secondary citadel was built in the southwest corner.

There were also gardens, a central canal, and a huge mound, which was planted with trees and meant to imitate a mountain landscape. However, the city was not completed when Sargon died, and it soon became obsolete.

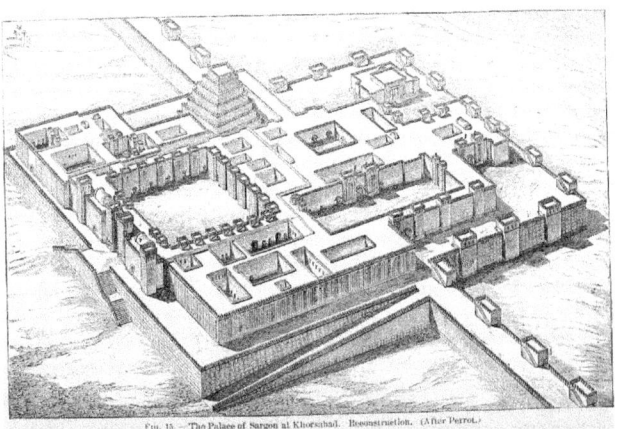

A 1905 artist's impression of the palace at Dur-Sharrukin.[11]

Sargon appeared to have relied a great deal on his close family, such as Crown Prince Sennacherib and his brother and grand vizier, Sin-ahu-usur. Perhaps this, together with the move to Dur-Sharrukin, reflects a feeling of insecurity on Sargon's part. He clearly did not relish the prospect of opposition to his plans in Ashur or Kalhu.

Under Sargon, deportations or resettlements became an even larger feature of Assyrian policy. He deported as many as 600,000 people, seeding new provinces with Assyrians while resettling many of the population of Samaria (conquered in 722) to Assyria. Many of the deportees probably ended up in the region where Dur-Sharrukin was located, working on construction projects or working on new farms. One rebellion in a border area saw five thousand people relocated into the Assyrian heartlands after the insurgency had been put down.

There were three different kinds of provinces in the Assyrian Empire:

- The heartland, where city governors ruled on the king's behalf;
- The border marches to the north and northwest, which were governed by the king's closest officials;
- Annexed foreign lands, which were governed by Assyrian-appointed local rulers.

Assyria had reached the limits of its power. To the west was the Mediterranean, and to the south was the Arabian Desert, both of which presented barriers. The Zagros Mountains blocked the way to Iran. Assyria had become a massive empire, but it faced geographical limits that it was powerless to overcome.

A year after moving to Dur-Sharrukin, Sargon set out on a campaign to Anatolia. He must have been sixty by that point, and he was accustomed to military success. He could have let a general take control of the campaign, but perhaps he had no one he could trust, or perhaps he felt he was invincible. This time, however, he had miscalculated. The enemy broke into his camp, found him, and killed him. Worse, from the Assyrian point of view, his body could not be recovered. He would never join the other kings in the royal tombs of Ashur, and his ghost would wander the world without peace.

Sennacherib succeeded his father, Sargon, in 705. He never moved to Dur-Sharrukin. Maybe he saw it as unlucky, or maybe he thought it was haunted by Sargon's uneasy spirit. He did everything he could to distance himself from his father, whom he must have felt had been cursed. Unlike almost every other legitimate king of Assyria, he never mentioned his father's name in any of his inscriptions. He soon relocated the capital to Nineveh, which he rebuilt extensively.

Sennacherib spent immense amounts on the construction of his new capital, which covered nearly two thousand acres. Nineveh became more than twice the size of both the preceding capitals, Kalhu and Dur-Sharrukin, and was surrounded by a seven-and-a-half-mile-long wall.

Sennacherib's name means "the god Sin has replaced the brothers." This may indicate that he was a long-awaited son since Sargon's other children died in infancy. Later sources state that Sennacherib was afflicted by a demon. The loss of his father might have led to depression. This would make sense; if Sennacherib was a much-longed-for replacement, his father must have been very close to him.

A relief of Sennacherib.[18]

In many ways, Sennacherib can be regarded as the great consolidator who followed Sargon's expansion. He presented himself as a great innovator, an architectural and agricultural inventor, and a metallurgist, who increased the amount of tin used to create bronze. In his palace, he had the sculptors suppress the "extra leg" of the *lamassu*; before this point, they had been shown with four legs on each side, as if they were two reliefs folded together so that when seen at an angle, they appear to have five legs. The new treatment was perhaps less impressive, but it was more naturalistic.

Sennacherib not only rebuilt Nineveh; he also created a huge network of canals around the city. This appears to have developed in four phases, starting relatively small but becoming increasingly ambitious. This construction project included aqueducts, canals, and sluices. Many of the watercourses were subterranean. They were dug into the bedrock and accessed through vertical shafts every forty yards or so. (This kind of channel is still used in parts of the Arabian Peninsula, known as the *qanat* or *falaj*.)

A type of Archimedes screw was used instead of the primitive shaduf (a pivoting pole raising a bucket) to bring water up from one level to another. This was a massive innovation. To make the point about the king's control of the water, relief carvings were often made in the rock next to sluices or wells, showing the king as a patron.

Sennacherib also expressed royal ideology by bringing trees from other parts of the empire to the palace and creating a marsh to imitate the Babylonian marshland. He had brought the extreme ends of the empire to Nineveh. He also planted fruit trees of all kinds, an assertion of fertility that might have referred to the sacred tree shown in Ashurnasirpal's reliefs.

Sennacherib took the title of king of Babylon, going one step further than his father, who only took the title of viceroy; the god Marduk had been recognized as the real king of the city. This could not have gone down well with the Babylonians. Furthermore, Sennacherib didn't turn up for the rite of taking Marduk's hand as his father had done. This was one of Sargon's mistakes that came back to haunt the Assyrian Empire.

A rebellion broke out in Babylon. It probably could have been suppressed quite easily, but Marduk-apla-iddina, sitting comfortably in exile in Elam, saw his chance. He headed straight for Babylon, got rid of the leader of the rebellion, and took control. And this time, thanks to making himself agreeable while in exile, he had backing from Elam.

Sennacherib was forced to invade. The very sensible Marduk-apla-iddina ran to the marshes again. Sennacherib appointed Bel-ibni, a young Babylonian and a hostage who "had grown up like a puppy in my palace" as the new king.[i] Sennacherib plundered Babylon. Perhaps he was determined to do exactly what his father would not have done.

After Bel-ibni proved incapable of suppressing rebellions in the south of his domains (according to some accounts, he actually joined them), Sennacherib replaced him. This time, he kept things in the family, giving his eldest son, Ashur-nadin-shumi, the throne of Babylon.

Then, Sennacherib turned to the Levant. Several Philistine rulers had stopped paying tribute, so a punitive expedition was needed. Sennacherib took Sidon, whose king had fled without defending his city; Ashkelon, where the king was taken captive and sent to Assyria; Ekron; and Lachish, where the siege lasted so long that the archers ran out of metal arrowheads.

Finally, in 701, he blockaded Jerusalem. As usual, diplomacy was tried first. 2 Kings 18 NKJV tells how Sennacherib's *rabshakeh* (chief cup-bearer or vizier) promises the Hebrews that if they join Assyria and leave King Hezekiah, they will receive special treatment. "Make peace with me by a present and come out to me," he says, "and every one of you eat from his own vine and every one from his own fig tree, and every one of you drink the waters of his own cistern; until I come and take you away to a land like your own land, a land of grain and new wine, a land of bread and vineyards, a land of olive groves and honey, that you may live and not die."

This was the way Assyria saw deportation; it was not a punishment but an organized and useful way of settling people on land that could sustain them and support the Assyrian Empire. The ultimate goal was to create a homogeneous "Assyrian" population. Intermarriage was encouraged.

In any case, this promise was not acceptable to the people of Israel, and Sennacherib could not take Jerusalem. However, the blockade worked. Hezekiah eventually decided to pay tribute, and Sennacherib walked away. Or, at least, that's the Assyrian version. There is a rather different ending in the Bible. Instead of Sennacherib making a

---

[i] Radner, Karen. *Ancient Assyria: A Very Short Introduction.* Oxford University Press, Oxford, 2015.

diplomatic decision, God intervened, striking 185,000 Assyrian soldiers dead in the night.

There is something of a puzzle one has to work out when reconciling the two accounts. Perhaps the Hebrews simply didn't believe Sennacherib would give up unless he had to. Sennacherib had probably weighed up the cost of a protracted siege at a time when food resources were becoming stretched, and this enabled a negotiated settlement that both sides could claim as a victory.

In 694, Sennacherib decided to tackle an old enemy, taking a military force to Elam. This would allow him to root out those Babylonian rebels who had escaped to Elam. The Assyrian forces crossed the Persian Gulf on boats crewed by Phoenicians and Greeks. The Assyrians were not a maritime people, but the empire's expansion had brought new skilled workers, and Sennacherib decided to apply them for the first time in warfare. This was a great success, as he conquered a number of Elamite cities.

However, this had unexpected results. The king of Elam, seeing how far Sennacherib was from his capital, decided to go on the offensive and invaded Babylon. The anti-Assyrian faction in Babylon decided to play one enemy off against the other. They handed Ashur-nadin-shumi, their Assyrian-imposed king and the Assyrian crown prince, to the Elamites. He was taken to Elam, and he disappeared from history.

Sennacherib set out for vengeance. He took the new Babylonian king, Nergal-ushezib, captive and brought him to Nineveh. Nergal-ushezib was chained to a wild bear at the gate of the citadel. (This might have been the Assyrians' idea of entertainment.) Sennacherib then invaded Elam for a second time. Though he had success early on, he wasn't prepared for the Persian mountain winter and turned back before being able to end the campaign. The inscriptions in which Sennacherib talks about this journey show very clearly how terrifying the rugged, snowy mountains and passes were for men used to the flat, open steppes of Assyria.

Sennacherib realized he would have to defeat both Elam and Babylon to be secure since the two states would always support each other against him. In 691, an anti-Assyrian coalition of Elamites and Babylonians was put together, and they moved north along the Tigris to threaten Ashur. But Sennacherib was ready for them. At Halule (modern Samarra), he managed to block their advance, and by the following year, he had moved his army south to besiege Babylon. It took fifteen months before the city fell. Sennacherib's troops plundered Babylon, massacred the population, and destroyed the city and its irrigation system. Babylon was no more. This was Sennacherib's fourth campaign against Babylon, and he had finally succeeded in destroying the threat to Assyria.

However, to secure the political achievement, the gods had to be brought into play to affirm the conquest in the divine sphere as well as the earthly sphere. That meant that Babylon's gods had to be absorbed into the Assyrian religion. Sennacherib had Marduk's throne and bed brought to Ashur, and he erected an "Akitu house" modeled on the Babylonian one in Ashur. (The Akitu house is a temple visited by the god Marduk at the New Year festival.) It even included earth taken from the ruins of Babylon in its foundations. Ashur had eaten up Marduk, and Assyria had swallowed Babylon.

Sennacherib never took the title of king of Babylon (again doing the opposite of what his father had done), so the city was left without a ruler.

Sennacherib had probably spent more time out of Assyria than in it by this point, and he might have lost his grasp of domestic politics. Since the crown prince, Ashur-nadin-shumi, had likely been executed in Elam, Sennacherib made Urdu-Mullissi (also written as Arda-Mulissu) crown prince. However, in 684 BCE, he suddenly changed his mind. Sennacherib instead promoted a younger son, Esarhaddon, to the post. Why Esarhaddon? Some historians blame Naqia, his mother, for influencing Sennacherib. Esarhaddon was a mature man when he was chosen, so perhaps he had managed to prove himself to his father.

For a couple of years, things seemed to settle down. Then, for whatever reason, Esarhaddon was sent away from Nineveh to a "secret place." This was most likely intended to ensure his safety. It did not, however, ensure Sennacherib's safety. In October 681 BCE, Urdu-Mullissi and his brother Nabu-shar-usur decided to act. 2 Kings 19 NIV tells the story:

"So Sennacherib king of Assyria broke camp and withdrew. He returned to Nineveh and stayed there. One day, while he was worshiping in the temple of his god Nisrok, his sons Adrammelek and Sharezer killed him with the sword, and they escaped to the land of Ararat. And Esarhaddon his son succeeded him as king."

Esarhaddon, though exiled, was able to march on Nineveh and take the throne. He made sure that everything was done correctly. He was invested as king in Ashur, which remained the religious capital and the home of the god from whom the king of Assyria held his authority. If Sennacherib had been punished for his blasphemy against Marduk and his destruction of the temples in Babylon, Esarhaddon was going to ensure that at least the god Ashur was on his side.

He then got rid of the entire palace security detail. State officials who might have supported his brother were sacked or executed. For the rest of his reign, Esarhaddon was an uneasy man. He regularly asked the oracle of Shamash whether anyone was planning to rebel against him. (His successor, Ashurbanipal, asked the oracle about a number of military operations and political decisions, but Ashurbanipal never seemed to have asked about rebellions. Perhaps he didn't feel he needed to.) Esarhaddon created a state of high vigilance, used agents provocateurs, and encouraged denunciations. His Assyria was, in many ways, a surveillance state.

There were, indeed, rebellions in a number of Assyrian towns, just as Esarhaddon had suspected. His foreign military success contrasted with the unease and plotting at home. Yet, Esarhaddon survived all the plots.

In 677, he seized Sidon and executed its king. He then made a treaty with Tyre. In 674, he made a treaty with Elam, ending the rivalry between the two states and thus securing the eastern border. This allowed him to set his sights on the west and Egypt, which was then ruled by the Nubian (Kushite) dynasty.

Esarhaddon's first attempt on Egypt, in 673 BCE, was a failure, which made him unpopular at home. However, he gathered new allies and attacked Egypt again two years later from Sinai. This time, he was more successful and managed to conquer Egypt as far south as Thebes (about halfway to Egypt's southern border). Egypt became, effectively, a vassal of Assyria since the Kushite King Taharqa fled the field. Esarhaddon installed vassal rulers in Memphis (modern-day Cairo) and Sais (located in the Nile Delta) and took his booty back to Ashur.

Esarhaddon was very unusual to the Egyptians. Every previous foreign ruler of Egypt had adopted the pharaonic titles and dress. The Macedonian Ptolemaic dynasty did so too. But Esarhaddon made no attempt at all to be a pharaoh. Maybe the culture was just too alien to him, or maybe the way Assyria managed vassal states made it unnecessary. Or maybe, having been given his crown by the god Ashur himself, Esarhaddon just didn't see the point of pretending to *be* a god.

Growing increasingly unpopular at home probably did nothing for Esarhaddon's paranoia. The cities of Nineveh and Kalhu became impregnable fortresses, and his obsession with state security continued. Then, in 670, Esarhaddon carried out another purge of his courtiers and officials after an episode of opposition to his rule in northern Syria. The Babylonian Chronicles say, "The king put his officers to the sword in Assyria." It gives no further detail. However, the purge must have been savage. For the first time, there was no high official in place whose name could be used as the eponym for the year's name. It is likely that Ashur-nasir, the chief eunuch who had led the Egyptian campaign, was one of those killed. He was killed just a year after his triumph.

Letters from Esarhaddon's exorcist (who filled roughly the same role as a doctor or psychiatrist would today) suggest that the king was clinically depressed following the death of his wife Esharra-hammat and their baby child. He might have had a form of post-traumatic stress disorder stemming from the assassination of his father.

One sign of Esarhaddon's increasing disturbance was his use of an ancient rite to escape his duties. A substitute king could be used to protect the king from the dangers that came about during a solar eclipse; for a hundred days, a substitute took the king's place. This was intended to blindside the forces of chaos and ensure that, following the eclipse, the king could regain his throne unharmed with no danger to the governance of the Assyrian state.

But Esarhaddon used the rite at least four times, including just a few days after his first victory in Egypt. He didn't use the rite to avoid eclipses; rather, he wanted to be able to hide away from his position as king and retreat into private life. Because he used this ritual, everyone was happy except for the substitute king, who was always killed at the end of the hundred days. Esarhaddon, who was clearly a smart guy, managed to choose political rivals for the position of substitute king.

Under Esarhaddon, Assyria became even more multiethnic and multicultural. Assyrian priests and scholars were joined by Babylonians, and his new conquests saw an Egyptian doctor and Egyptian astronomers and priests join his court.

Sennacherib had a tense relationship with his dead father, and Esarhaddon had a strange relationship with his father. Convinced that Sennacherib had been targeted by the gods for his plunder of Babylon, Esarhaddon set about rebuilding the capital his father had destroyed.

The rebuilding of Babylon was Esarhaddon's big building program, rivaling Dur-Sharrukin and Nineveh. For the first time, an Assyrian king funded a huge construction project outside of Assyria, and for the first time, it was funded from outside Assyria too, at least partly. The tribute from Egypt helped pay for the work.

The first stage of construction was clearance. The city had to be cleared of the vegetation that had invaded it, and the river had to be re-channeled into its original course before the area around the city had been flooded.

Assyria was a massive empire with seventy-five provinces. It was perhaps too big for one man to manage, so Esarhaddon decided to separate the two halves of his empire again. In 672, he made his younger son, Ashurbanipal, the crown prince of Ashur, and his older son, Shamash-shumu-ukin, became the crown prince of Babylon. This may seem unusual; surely, the younger son should have been sent to Babylon. An inscription shows why this was the case. Shamash-shumu-ukin was a kind of living sacrifice, a gift to Marduk and the goddess Zarpanitu, the gods of Babylon.

The succession agreement was widely disseminated on steles, in inscriptions, and even in the royal seal, which showed the scene of the king killing a lion in triplicate, representing the triple rule of Esarhaddon and the two princes. However, the demand that officials had to swear in a succession oath was purely to Ashurbanipal, whose mother was Assyrian. Shamash-shumu-ukin's mother was Babylonian.

Esarhaddon died in 669. He was on his way to Egypt again to put down a rebellion under Taharqa. He left an unfinished palace in Kalhu that was built in the Egyptian style. Ashurbanipal inherited a wealthy, successful empire, but there was a hidden death wound. Because of Esarhaddon's two great purges of the civil service, he had destroyed the administration's power to function.

Ashurbanipal (r. 669–631) continued the Assyrian expedition in Egypt. In 667, he invaded, reconquered the country, and installed Necho of Sais as a vassal ruler despite the fact that he had been involved in Taharqa's rebellion. Necho's son Psamtik was also given a high office.

The Kushite dynasty fought back a few years later. Taharqa's successor, Tantamani, surged up the Nile in a fresh offensive, and Necho was killed while defending Memphis. Psamtik fled, but he came back the next year, supported by Ashurbanipal and the Assyrian army.

Ashurbanipal swept through Egypt as far south as Thebes, which he sacked in 663, taking two obelisks back to Assyria, as well as many of the city's inhabitants and a vast amount of gold and silver. Although the archaeological evidence shows that the Assyrians took a good deal of loot, they did not burn the city or destroy buildings. Psamtik was then installed as pharaoh, although he only ruled the top half of Egypt. Ashurbanipal returned to Assyria.

Ashurbanipal probably saw Psamtik as a tame provincial ruler. However, Psamtik reunited Egypt. He founded the Twenty-sixth Dynasty and nearly outlived the Assyrian Empire.

Esarhaddon's succession agreement gave Ashurbanipal the senior role; though his brother was installed as king of Babylon, it was understood that Assyria was the senior kingship. This must have upset his brother, particularly since several major cities in Babylonia (Nippur, Uruk, and Ur) ignored him and dealt directly with Nineveh. After a decade and a half of dutiful administration of what Ashurbanipal saw as simply another Assyrian province, Shamash-shumu-ukin rebelled in 652. He was supported by Elam, though not by all his own subjects.

By 650, things were going wrong for Shamash-shumu-ukin. Ashurbanipal had driven him back, taking Sippar and Borsippa on the way, and was now able to lay siege to Babylon. According to Ashurbanipal's account, Babylon was so sore-pressed that the citizens had resorted to cannibalism, but exaggeration was a regular feature of Assyrian kings' inscriptions. Still, a two-year siege must have reduced living standards in Babylon significantly.

Eventually, the city fell. Ashurbanipal went on a rampage. His inscriptions are full of atrocities, such as carving up bodies to feed them to pigs and dogs. However, they don't say what happened to Shamash-shumu-ukin.

Perhaps the "Tale of the Two Brothers" has the answer. This story is known from a 4th-century Egyptian papyrus (written in both Aramaic and Demotic Egyptian) and tells how Ashurbanipal's and Shamash-shumu-ukin's sister, Sherua-etirat, pleads with her rebellious brother to submit to the king or to burn himself and his family on a pyre together with the Babylonian scholars who tempted him to rebel. He refuses, and when the temple of Marduk is set on fire, he dies in the flames.

Whatever happened to Shamash-shumu-ukin, Ashurbanipal had won. But four years of civil war had left Babylon destabilized and in famine, which destroyed the prestige of Assyria. Babylon, having been destroyed twice in living memory by Assyrian kings, simmered with hatred for its northern rivals.

Elam continued to be a thorn in Assyria's side despite a very successful earlier campaign against Teumman, who had been killed in the Battle of the Ulai River, giving Ashurbanipal a chance to install his own choice of rulers. (Teumman was decapitated; the scene is shown in nauseating detail in the reliefs in Ashurbanipal's palace, and the inscriptions boast of making the rivers run red with blood.) But revolt after revolt occurred in Elam. By 646, Ashurbanipal had decided it was time to put an end to the Elamite problem.

Ashurbanipal probably went further on this campaign than any previous Assyrian king. He might have even taken tribute from some of the Iranian kingdoms. On his way back, he decided to destroy the Elamite capital, Susa. He demolished the temples and the ziggurat, sacked the palace, and "god-napped" no fewer than nineteen Elamite gods. The royal tombs of Elam were destroyed, and the king of Elam was taken to Nineveh, where he had to pull Ashurbanipal's chariot.

The events recounted in these inscriptions appear to justify Frahm's assessment of Ashurbanipal as a "scholar, sadist, hunter, king."[i] Ashurbanipal was proud of his image as a hunter. Reliefs in Ashurbanipal's palace show him killing eighteen lions, which perhaps was a "magic number" since Nineveh has eighteen gates (a lion could protect each of the gates of the city). Ashurbanipal apparently had an arena built specially for lion hunting. The lions might have been sedated.

Ashurbanipal also presented himself as a scholar. This was not unusual in Assyria, as kings were well educated and frequently looked to the past as a precedent for their exploits. The Library of Ashurbanipal at Nineveh was impressive. There were clay tablets and numerous wax tablets. The latter was lost in a fire, but the heat baked and preserved the clay tablets.

Although the library included the only complete text of the *Epic of Gilgamesh*, its key documents concerned rituals, oracles, omens, astrology, and divination. These texts provided materials that could support the king's decision-making. Ashurbanipal not only had scholarly

---

[i] Frahm, Eckart. *Assyria: The Rise and Fall of the World's First Empire.* Basic Books, New York, 2023.

astrological texts, but he also sponsored astrologers to study and record celestial phenomena in what one might call a more scientific way.

The library was also multilingual. It contained Assyrian texts, the Babylonian epic of creation, and texts in Babylonian, Assyrian, and the ancient Sumerian language.

Ashurbanipal was the most erudite of royal collectors, but he inherited much of his library from earlier rulers, maybe as early as Ashur-uballit I. Tukulti-Ninurta I added Babylonian texts to the library, one of the results of his conquest of Babylon.

Still, life was good for the Assyrians during Ashurbanipal's reign. Excavations of the western capital of Dur-Katlimmu show how Shulmu-sharri, a wealthy man, enjoyed his life in the Red House, with its four courtyards, two floors, two wells, and an effective sewage and drainage system. He had many slaves and three adult sons. In his fifties, he became a "companion" of Ashurbanipal, which was an accredited representative of the king. His house gives a good idea of the luxury in which the truly wealthy of the Neo-Assyrian Empire were able to live.

Ashur's traders voyaged along the Tigris to buy wine in Syria. They brought it back on rafts made of Syrian wood and sold it for timber when they arrived in Assyria. By this time, Assyria held territory all the way from the Mediterranean to the Persian Gulf; it was the unrivaled superpower of its time.

But this was not to last. Perhaps climate change was partly responsible; agricultural yields headed downward again, and elephants became extinct in the region. Perhaps Esarhaddon's purges had led to poor governance and a decline in public infrastructure. The eponym year list ends in 639, and there is a surprising lack of documentation for the last years of Ashurbanipal's reign, suggesting that communications were breaking down.

Perhaps delusions of grandeur were the worst problems that Assyria had to deal with. The economy was starting to teeter, but Ashurbanipal was not paying attention. The market price for grain (calculated from comparing a number of transfer documents) appeared to have been over a thousand times more than the official price. Grain shortages and high inflation forced poor people to sell their children or give them as pledges for loans. However, for the wealthy and for the government, the golden age was still alive and well.

So, when things went wrong, they went wrong very quickly.

In 631 or 630 BCE, Ashurbanipal died or was deposed. Again, there is very limited information; the records were not being kept up to date at this point. He was succeeded by his son, Ashur-etil-ilani, who reigned for three years. Sinsharishkun, another son of Ashurbanipal, then claimed the throne, but this was disputed for some time by the chief eunuch despite the fact that, according to Assyrian tradition, a eunuch was ineligible to rule.

This leadership crisis gave the anti-Assyrian faction in Babylon the opportunity it needed. Nabopolassar, whose origins are unknown, took the throne of Babylon and went on the offensive. There was a battle to the death between Assyria and Babylon.

These battles might have continued indefinitely, but the arrival of a new power, the Medes, to the east changed things. The Iranian tribes had spent 150 years living as fragmented tribes, but they eventually created a confederacy that was able to work together on campaigns. In 614, they captured Ashur, burning the city (this is confirmed by the archaeological record). Ashur's temple, which gave the kings of Assyria their legitimacy, was destroyed, as were the tombs of the kings.

Nabopolassar quickly allied himself with the Medes. Their goal was obvious: to capture the capital of the Assyrian Empire, Nineveh.

In 612, Nineveh fell. King Sinsharishkun disappeared without a trace (it is assumed that he was killed in the battle), and Nineveh appeared to have been abandoned. The soldiers who died defending the Shamash Gate of the city were never buried. Images of the Assyrian kings were disfigured. Their eyes were scratched out, and their noses were broken off. The city was looted and then destroyed. Babylonian engineers redirected Sennacherib's canals to destroy the mudbrick walls of the citadel. Kalhu, too, was completely wrecked and then abandoned. Bodies were thrown into the wells to poison the water and make the city uninhabitable. Irrigation works were destroyed, making it impossible to farm the land. Assyria was in ruins.

With Ashur destroyed, no new king could be rightfully invested. Ashur-uballit II performed his ceremony of investiture at Harran in 612, but it seemed that many considered him only the crown prince. With Egyptian support, he continued an Assyrian state in exile in Harran (far to the north on the modern border between Syria and Turkey). In 610, Babylon managed to take Harran, and the last inscription to mention

Ashur-uballit II dates to 609. He simply disappeared from history after that date, and with him, the Assyrian Empire came to an end. It only took twenty-one years after Ashurbanipal's death for the empire to end.

Nabopolassar and his son Nebuchadnezzar II deported many Assyrians to Babylonia, adopting the Assyrian custom of resettlement. The Neo-Babylonian Empire was on the rise. It even managed to defeat the Egyptians.

Strangely enough, the god Ashur was still worshiped in his temple on the crag overlooking the Tigris under the Persian Achaemenid Empire, which saw an economic, though not political, resurgence in Assyria and later under the Parthians. It was only around 240 CE that the Sasanians captured and sacked Ashur, finally destroying the temple.

Chapter 8: Language Diversity

Ashurbanipal claimed that "Ashur has placed at my disposal all the languages that are spoken from sunrise to sunset."[i] For once, he was not exaggerating, or at least not much. Assyria was a multilinguistic kingdom right from the start.

Assyria inherited a classical language. Sumerian was a language isolate, meaning it was not related to any other languages. It was also the first written language. However, it is important to realize that our knowledge of Sumerian is refracted through Akkadian. Even the name "Sumerian" is Akkadian; the language was *emegir* or "native tongue" to its speakers.

The cuneiform characters in which the language was written started as rough pictographs. Then, the marks became abstract and wedge-shaped, made with a reed stylus pressed into clay. It must have been quite fast to write, particularly compared with Egyptian hieroglyphics. Originally a logographic system, where each sign was a word, it became a mixed system in which the signs could be used for individual syllables. This is similar to modern Japanese, which uses a syllabary together with kanji, Chinese characters that represent a word.

The process of cuneiform development occurred slowly over time, taking at least from 2800 (when the first syllabic signs are dated to but are rare) to 2600 BCE (when they became relatively common). Some signs

---

[i] Frahm, Eckart. *Assyria: The Rise and Fall of the World's First Empire*. Basic Books, New York, 2023.

were also used as unspoken determinatives, that is, signs that denoted what kind of thing the word described. For instance, gods' names were given a star.

The Rassam cylinder, a cuneiform historical document.[14]

List making was an obsession of Sumerian scribal culture, and it remained an important facet of post-Sumerian Mesopotamian culture too. There were lists of trees, lists of animals, lists of professions, and so on. Many of these lists were still being copied hundreds of years after Sumerian had died out as a spoken language.

Hymns often remained in Sumerian even at a late date, though they would have become obscure by then. This is similar to the way Latin was used until the 1950s in Catholic Mass. To help priests who might not have been fluent in Sumerian, some texts had a translation in Assyrian inserted between the lines.

Fluency in written Sumerian was essential for scholars, though. "What kind of scribe is a scribe who does not know Sumerian?" asks a text written four thousand years ago.[i]

The next language to arrive was Akkadian. This was a Semitic language, like Hebrew, Arabic, Aramaic, and some of the Ethiopian languages (Tigrinya and Amharic). It was completely unrelated to Sumerian. Old Assyrian documents are often written in Akkadian.

Both Assyrian and Babylonian developed out of Akkadian, and both languages are sometimes described as Akkadian dialects. They are similar but distinct. Both languages used cuneiform script, though the scripts are not exactly the same. An expert can easily distinguish the two languages just from the writing without reading the words. The Babylonian script was less legible than the more regular Assyrian script. Ashurbanipal had a number of Babylonian texts copied into the Assyrian script.

Reading cuneiform remains a challenge. Different signs can have the same phonetic value, a bit like how "gh," "f," and "ph" can all be read as "f" (such as in the words "enough," "fish," and "phonetic"). However, one sign can have multiple readings. The ability to use signs for concepts, words, and sounds continues. Intriguingly, cuneiform became more complex during the Middle Assyrian period and even more complex during the Neo-Assyrian period, perhaps due to the fact that highly educated scribes felt the need to stress the importance of their profession.

During the Middle Assyrian period, Babylonian—the more prestigious of the languages—was often used for official texts. Under Tukulti-Ninurta II, inscriptions were written in an Assyrian dialect, eschewing Babylonian words and phrases. This constituted a strong assertion of national identity as Assyria fought its way back from chaotic times. Clearly, language was a weapon in the culture wars between Babylonia and Assyria.

During the Old Babylonian period, Sumerian remained the literary and scholarly language. A number of bilingual tablets have been found,

---

[i] Crawford, Harriet. *The Sumerian World*. Routledge, London and New York, 2013. Pg. 95.

such as a list of geographical names in both Sumerian and Akkadian or Assyrian, from which scribes would learn their trade or which they might use for reference.

During the 1st millennium BCE, things changed. Assyrian remained the official language, but Aramaic (another Semitic language) became the language of daily life. Its use began as a commercial language and then spread throughout the empire. However, very few records from Assyrian times survive that are written in Aramaic. There is a reason for this. Assyrian texts were written on clay tablets, but Aramaic was written on leather or papyrus sheets. Most of the Aramaic texts we have come from much later times and were preserved in the Judean Desert, not in Mesopotamia.

It is interesting that several reliefs show pairs of scribes. One of them is shown writing with a pen on a scroll and the other with a stylus on a tablet. The tablet might be made of clay for a permanent record or of wax for temporary notes or calculations that could later be erased. (The wax holders survived in a few cases, with the more luxurious ones being carved out of ivory, but the wax they contained was destroyed by time.)

Aramaic, unlike Assyrian, was written in an alphabetic script that descended from the Phoenician alphabet and was written from right to left (Assyrian went from left to right). Aramaic is still spoken today by Assyrian Christians in the Middle East and in the Assyrian diaspora. Confusingly, it is referred to as "modern Assyrian." It is very distantly related to the Assyrian of Ashurbanipal's day; it would be similar to the relationship between German and modern American English.

One tablet found at Nineveh contains a scribe's speculation on the original forms of later Assyrian cuneiform characters. They are not correct but show that the Assyrians were aware of the long history of their language and were interested in discovering more about it.

Aramaic is not often found on monuments, but Shalmaneser III's palace has Aramaic characters painted on the glazed bricks, probably as a guide to where the bricks needed to go. The bricklayers, or at least the construction manager, might have been able to read or at least identify Aramaic characters but not cuneiform. Aramaic summaries are often appended to the formal Assyrian texts regarding contracts for property sales, and clay tablets in Aramaic were used as IOUs or debt notes.

Literacy appears to have been widespread. Many adult freemen and some women could read. There were more literate people in the

Assyrian Empire than in most other societies of the time. Basic literacy could be achieved with the knowledge of just 80 to 120 cuneiform characters in Old Assyrian times; people learning other Middle Eastern scripts had to learn a lot more characters. In Egypt, the use of hieroglyphs limited literacy to a very small percentage of the population. At least 750 hieroglyphs would be needed for even basic communication.

Excavations have found cuneiform tablets in about a third of private houses in Ashur. These are often business documents, but religious and literary texts have been found too. Literacy was widespread in other towns of the empire, both in cuneiform and in the alphabetic Aramaic script.

Kings not only read but also often had editions of scholarly books in their personal libraries. While Ashurbanipal maybe wasn't as great a scholar as he thought, kings were educated well enough to make use of them. Esarhaddon, for instance, often wrote to his scholars for clarification of tricky passages or potential misunderstandings and ambiguities. He obviously paid close attention to the texts he read.

Throughout the Assyrian and Babylonian Empires, there was a great respect for the written word, and it was used to achieve permanence. For instance, the Code of Hammurabi was inscribed on a stele and copied frequently. Copying the code actually became part of the regular curriculum for scribes in training, with the practice still being around a thousand years later. (There was a copy of the Code of Hammurabi in the Library of Ashurbanipal.)

In Ashurnasirpal II's palace, each of the relief panels has the middle portion of the sculpture overwritten with what has become known as the Standard Inscription, which praises the king as the king of the world, priest, and ruler chosen by the gods. The inscription is cut into the relief, so it was clearly done after the relief was carved. The relief would have been considered incomplete without it. (Today, we would be more likely to think that a sculpture has been ruined if something was written over it.)

However, though there was immense respect for the written word in Assyria, there appeared to have been less respect for professional scribes. They never made as much money as traders. One text says,

"The house of the chief scribe is miserable, a donkey wouldn't go in there!"[i]

Finally, it is worth stressing that, particularly in the Neo-Assyrian Empire, we often know kings by the Hebrew version of their names, not by their actual kingly names. Tiglath-Pileser, for instance, was named in Assyrian as Tukulti-apil-Esharra, "I trust in the son of Esharra" (the god Ninurta, son of Ashur, whose temple was called Esharra - "world-temple").

Shalmaneser was a name only ever given to kings and might have been taken only after coming to power. Shalmaneser V was referred to as Ululayu when he was a prince. Again, Shalmaneser is the biblical version; the Assyrian name would have been Shalmanu-ashared, "Shalman is foremost" or "the friendly one is foremost," possibly referring to a manifestation of Ashur. (Intriguingly, the name appears to be related to the Hebrew name Solomon.)

Assyrian is widely considered a dead language. However, Babylonian is not fully dead yet. The first film in Babylonian came out just a few years ago. "The Poor Man of Nippur" was made in 2018 by Cambridge University's Department of Assyriology and tells the comical tale of a poor man getting his revenge on the lazy, sleazy mayor of his city. This story was found on a clay tablet that dates to around 710 BCE. If you would like to see it, it's on YouTube and features a rather lovable (though doomed) goat, as well as some Oscar-level slapstick!

---

[i] Elayi, Josette. *Esarhaddon, King of Assyria*. Lockwood Press, Columbus, Georgia, 2023.

Chapter 9: Religion and Beliefs

The Assyrian religion had much in common with the religions of the rest of Mesopotamia, though some of the details differ. It was a polytheistic religion in which many gods were associated with natural phenomena (sun, moon, storms, etc.) or with particular places.

One of the big themes of religion in Mesopotamia was the conflict between chaos and order. Chaos is what was there before the world. It was often described as a deep abyss or total darkness. The people saw it as a threat that had to be tamed. In the Babylonian creation myth, chaos was represented by Tiamat, goddess of the sea, who gave birth to monsters until she was killed by the god Marduk. After dividing her in two, Marduk separated heaven and earth, creating order out of chaos. He made her ribs into the vault of heaven, and her eyes shed tears that became the Tigris and Euphrates. (In Assyrian versions, it is Ashur who killed Tiamat.)

The figure of the king killing a lion is prevalent in Assyrian art, as it was part of the royal seal. This is a replay of the battle between chaos and order and recreates scenes of the gods killing monstrous creatures.

The myth of the Great Flood, similar to the flood Noah faced in the Bible, is found in Sumerian mythology and was certainly known to the Assyrians. Like Tiamat, the Great Flood symbolized the destructive power of water. Perhaps Sennacherib's destruction of Babylon by opening the sluices was meant to reflect the flood myth.

Demons and monsters were ever-present forces of chaos against which protection needed to be sought from the gods or guardian spirits.

The great human-headed winged bulls called *lamassu*, for instance, didn't just form impressive entrances to a king's palace. They also acted as magical protectors. Incantations could also be used to ward off demons.

Lamashtu was an incarnation of chaos. This demon had a lion's head, bird's claws, and a woman's body and sagging breasts. Lamashtu killed young children and sometimes killed mothers in childbirth. To protect against this, expectant mothers made clay figures of Lamashtu and sent them down the Tigris to "send her away."

Pazuzu was the king of the wind demons. He had a lion's face and clawed hands and feet. However, he could be used as a source of good magic, and his figure was often carved on amulets. Other protectors included Ugallu, "great lion," and the urmahlullu, "lion man," who wore bull horns on the front of his helmet as a divine symbol. Lahmu were depicted as bearded men with hair in flowing ringlets. Images of Lahmu are inscribed with the phrase, "Enter, spirit of peace; depart, spirit of evil!" The Apkallu had fish skin cloaks and a fish head as a helmet. They sometimes had bird heads and wings. They were protective spirits despite their monstrous looks.

The importance of demons made exorcism a standard procedure in Assyria since illnesses could be caused by demons or evil magic. The king had his own exorcist, which Assyrians would have seen as no stranger than a CEO nowadays having a therapist.

Magic was practiced by the *mashmashu* or *ashipu*. Magical incantations and spells have been preserved in writings. Amulets could be worn or hung on the wall of a house, and magical figurines were often buried in the foundations. Clay dogs were common foundation figures; they perhaps represented the protective nature of guard dogs. Burning a figurine might be seen as a form of magic. Incantations could be used to rid oneself of witchcraft or evil spirits.

The Assyrians believed in an afterlife of sorts. The underworld was the place where all the dead resided, virtuous or not. The dead ate dust and were blind and powerless. There was no heaven and no hell. All humans were mortal, and their days were numbered. This outlook must have been somewhat depressing.

Although there was no paradise to look forward to, having a decent burial was extremely important, partly to ensure that the dead were happy and did not come back as vengeful ghosts. (A Jewish legend tells how the son of the Babylonian monarch Nebuchadnezzar cut his body into three hundred pieces and fed them to the birds to ensure he could never return.) Houses and palaces had burial chambers in the basement. These were usually vaulted chambers with steps down so that the dead could be visited and given offerings. Grave goods included letters and other documents, jewelry, ivory combs and pins, and carved stone containers.

What was distinctive about Assyria was the god Ashur, the ruler of the city that took his name. Unlike most of the Mesopotamian gods, he did not (originally) have a wife or son. He was not even shown in human form; he was identified with the rock on which his temple was built. He was sometimes known as "lord of the mountain." In contrast, all the Babylonian gods are related to each other. They also all symbolize particular aspects of life, whereas Ashur was, quite simply, the power of the city, nothing else. He has no story; he is just a god of power and omnipotence.

The god Ashur in a winged disk.[15]

Other cities had their own deities. Babylon had the god Marduk, Nippur had the god Enlil, and Arbela had the goddess Ishtar. As Assyria expanded, it indulged in "god-napping," seizing foreign gods' cult statues and relocating them to Ashur in a supernatural equivalent of the resettlement of conquered populations.^i There was even a divine directory of Ashur telling priests where they could find the relevant god; it was a sort of telephone book of the gods.

Ashur's temple was called "Wild Bull: in the time of Erishum I, which suggests that Ashur might have originally been identified with that animal. Ashur was represented on one seal as a four-legged bull-headed rock. He was not given a temple outside the city of Ashur; instead, his weapons were venerated as the "sword of Ashur."

The king had an important part to play in the worship of Ashur, as he was the only go-between for his people. All hymns and prayers to Ashur mention the king prominently. This was not the case, for instance, with Ishtar, who was not a state god of Assyria.

Under Shamsi-Adad I, Ashur came to be conflated with Enlil of Nippur, the chief deity of the Sumerian pantheon. Enlil was known as "wild bull" and "great mountain." Both epithets could also be applied to Ashur. Eamkurkurra, "House, Wild Bull of All Lands," was the name of the new temple that Shamsi-Adad erected. (Hammurabi similarly raised Babylon's city god Marduk in status by stating that Enlil had transferred his powers to Marduk.)

From at least Shamsi-Adad's time, the palace and the temple of Ashur were connected. Other gods, though, were venerated on the other side of the palace toward the city. Even after the royal residence had been relocated to Kalhu and later to Nineveh, the kings of Assyria would come back to Ashur for the spring festival. When they died, they were buried under the old royal palace. The way the kings relied on Ashur is easy to see from the following inscription.

"Sennacherib the great king, mighty king, king of the world, king of Assyria, king of the four quarters, the wise, expert, heroic warrior, foremost among all rulers, the bridle that curbs the disobedient, and the one who smites the enemy with lightning. Ashur, the great god, gave me a kingship without rival; against all those who sit on thrones he made my weapons strong; from the upper sea to the lower sea, he made all the rulers of the world bow down at my feet."[ii]

---

[i] Radner, Karen. *Ancient Assyria: A Very Short Introduction*. Oxford University Press, Oxford, 2015.

[ii] Cotterell, Arthur. *The First Great Powers: Babylon and Assyria*. Hurst & Company, London, 2019. Pg. 121.

The Great Goddess might have been the main divinity worshiped in all the Assyrian cities at an early date. She was certainly well known in Sumer, where she was called Inanna. She became Ishtar in the Akkadian pantheon. In Babylon, she was known as "Ishtar the Assyrian," and she was the goddess of battle fury and sexual desire. She was sometimes called "the splendid lioness."

The goddess Ishtar shown on an Akkadian seal.[16]

Other gods included the following:

- Adad, the weather or storm god, who is sometimes represented by a triple thunderbolt. He was the son of Anum, the sky god. He was much more important in the dry steppes of Assyria than in Babylonia, which did not depend on rain for agricultural production.

- Sin, the moon god.
- Shamash, the sun god. Since he saw everything that happened each day, he was also the god of justice. He was known as Utu in Sumerian.
- Nabu, the god of writing and scribes. He was better known in Babylon than in Assyria.
- Ninurta started as a Sumerian god of grain. In Assyria, he became a warrior god and, as such, was often the patron of the king. Ninurta shot down the chaos eagle Anzu, who had stolen the tablets of destiny on which Enlil relied for his authority.

The gods required service from their worshipers, including sacrifices and libations. Even the earliest temples in Assyria included a blood basin, libation vessels from which beer could be poured, clay incense holders, and sacrificial bowls. Wheat, barley, sesame, fruit, and honey were presented to the gods, as well as meat by ritually pure priests who were clean-shaven (unlike other men, particularly the king).

Menus for the gods have been found on clay tablets, which show how far away some of the foodstuffs were sourced. Since everyone's work should nourish the gods, every Assyrian city and province had to send produce for offerings, which became an act of collective sacrifice. After the gods had taken their sustenance from the aromas, the foodstuffs were divided out among those present. This food was considered to have immense power. "Whoever eats the leftovers will live."[i]

Almost all rituals would have included beer, which had been associated with divinities from early on; intoxication was seen as a divine state.

Votive statues date from Sumerian times but have also been found in Assyrian temples. These figurines of worshipers with folded hands and huge eyes were probably set on mudbrick benches on the long sides of the sanctuary to represent their owners in permanent, unceasing prayer. The cult statue of the god would have been placed in a high, deep niche opposite the entrance, a plan that was found in the earliest temple at Ashur and does not seem to have changed much over the centuries. In the Neo-Assyrian Empire, rulers still set their statues up in such a

---

[i] Radner, Karen. *Ancient Assyria: A Very Short Introduction.* Oxford University Press, Oxford, 2015.

position that they could adore the god in the temple.

The use of oracles and divination is a characteristic of Mesopotamian religion. Omens were not absolutely determinative; however, they were an indicator of an elevated level of risk, which could be averted by taking action or by ritual or magic. Radner has pointed out that in an absolute monarchy, an oracle's answer to a question would have been a useful way to create debate.[i]

Queries might be addressed to Shamash or Adad in a number of ways. Extispicy—divination by examining the internal organs of sacrificed animals—was often used. Archaeologists have found a number of models of animal livers that were marked up so that diviners in training could practice their interpretations.

Other methods included astrology, the study of the weather, the interpretation of dreams, watching smoke from incense, or casting lots. Necromancy (asking questions of the dead) could be used, but this was considered risky. The importance of astrology was one major reason for the development of advanced mathematics; the Sumerians used both the decimal and the sexagesimal system (base sixty), and the Assyrians had tables of reciprocals, square roots, and cube roots.

Precise observation of nature was important. Tables were made of the daily change in the duration of the moon's visibility during the lunar month of the winter solstice, for example.

As one might expect in a culture with great regard for the written word, the questions were usually put in writing. One surviving tablet shows Esarhaddon inquiring of Shamash whether the appointment of Sin-nadin-apli as crown prince was acceptable and pleasing to the god. He also used extispicy to select which crafts workshops should be given commissions for rebuilding Babylonian temples.

Even the coronation ritual was written down. A 12th- or 11th-century BCE tablet described the procession of the monarch to Ashur's temple, where the proclamation "Ashur is king!" was made. After this, the king was addressed. "May Ashur put the crown on your head for a hundred years." At the end of the rite, the court officials gave up their emblems of power, and the king told them to resume their offices, thus ensuring the continued smooth functioning of the civil service. It is a fascinating

---

[i] Radner, Karen. *Ancient Assyria: A Very Short Introduction.* Oxford University Press, Oxford, 2015.

glimpse of how the religious and bureaucratic aspects of the Assyrian Empire functioned in tandem to ensure the state's continuation.

Chapter 10: Arts and Architecture

Assyria developed a highly stylized form of art and architecture that was intended to glorify its kings and gods. Art was intended to convey a message about the king's power and wealth and to impress Assyrians and visitors from outside the empire.

Buildings were constructed of mudbrick. There was no other viable choice since Assyria had few trees and very limited rock resources for building. Mudbrick building lends itself to accretion (adding on to or covering over earlier layers). At some sites, numerous different layers have been excavated under a single temple.

The main limitation on the size of buildings was the span of the ceiling beams that could be imported. Only smaller rooms might be vaulted. Beams were sometimes supported on terracotta or bronze-covered wooden fists ("hands of Ishtar"), which, oddly, had five fingers but no thumb. Gates and doors were made of wood and covered with metal bands, which might be highly decorated like the Balawat Gates of Shalmaneser III.

In the glaring sunlight of Mesopotamia, high and relatively narrow rooms were generally lit only by the doorways. This, together with the limits on roof spans, meant that most palaces were made up of various courtyards with large expanses of bare wall. The outside walls were often plastered with gypsum so that they shone gleaming white. The interior walls were decorated with glazed bricks, paint, and stone reliefs. Traces of paint remain on some of the carved stone friezes that survive from the royal palaces.

The palace would have looked like a long, horizontal mass. It was probably considerably higher than other secular buildings in the city. However, ziggurats, which were first developed by the Sumerians, introduced a more vertical focus. Since they were solid (filled with unfired mudbrick), their size was not limited in the same way as palace buildings. Buttresses on walls and ramps and staircases accessing the higher floors created strong accents that further emphasized their bulk.

The royal palaces from the time of Ashurnasirpal II were evidently designed to make an impact on visitors. Reliefs, cut into stone panels that must have been imported at some expense, would originally have been painted, at least partially. Soft Mosul marble—actually a kind of gypsum—is easy to work but hardens after exposure, which enabled Assyrian sculptors to create highly detailed works. On some of the reliefs, fine decorations are incised on the clothes to show the textile patterns of a brocade. There are floral patterns on the edge of the sleeve. A royal robe is decorated with sphinxes, winged bulls, trees of life, and the archetypal scene of the king killing a lion.

The subjects in the sculptures included scenes of subject peoples surrendering, battles, and tribute delivery, complete with a royal audience. Assyrian civility was shown as the assurance of order in a chaotic world. In the battle scenes, chaos is allowed to break out, but order is restored by the king, who is depicted as being in the presence of the god Ashur and his protective spirits.

Ashurbanipal's palace had particularly savage subjects. The scenes of the Battle of the Ulai River against the Elamites show one soldier sawing off the head of Teumman of Elam while another man picks up the royal hat, which has fallen on the ground. A later scene shows an Assyrian soldier waving the head from a chariot. Another scene shows Ashurbanipal lounging on a couch and his wife, Ashur-Sharrat, drinking with him in the garden, which is a highly civilized and very poised scene. However, on the left, a close look will detect the severed head of King Teumman hanging in the branches of a tree.

Ashurbanipal's banquet[17]

A number of conventions were developed. For instance, a fallen enemy (or lion or bull) would be shown beneath the wheels of the king's chariot. An odd form of perspective was used, in which the legs and head would be shown in profile, but the upper half of the body would be shown frontally. Cities were shown as a series of towers or crenelated buttresses. City walls were a sign of civilization and order, as well as a practical form of defense.

Sometimes, the conventions had a political message. No enemy chariots or cavalry are shown in any of Sargon's reliefs, even though his enemies did have these resources. The reliefs maintain the idea of Assyria being technologically and militarily superior.

The king was always shown as a perfect man in the prime of life. The muscles of arms and legs were exaggerated in Assyrian sculpture, and this was the case for animals as well as men. The king's long, curly beard is cut square across the bottom, and his long, curly hair comes down to his shoulders. He is always a figure of power, and in narrative scenes, he always has the grandest beard. Other nobles have shorter beards. Only very young men and eunuchs are shown with clean-shaven faces.

But perhaps the archetypal figures of Assyrian art are the colossal winged bulls and lions that guard the palace gates. They were usually made of a single piece of stone and could weigh up to thirty tons each. A relief from Sennacherib's time shows how they were dragged on sleds by teams of hundreds of men.

Despite the apparent similarity of Assyrian reliefs, connoisseurs have detected some differences between the art of different kings. Artwork made for Ashurnasirpal is impressive and detailed in high relief and very technically assured, while Tiglath-Pileser III commissioned slightly less impressive work in lower relief but with much more varied compositions and more detailed narratives. One room, in particular, showed all the main events of Tiglath-Pileser's reign; effectively, it was a graphic history of his achievements. However, almost all Assyrian work displays a dislike of empty space. Detail is always filled in; for instance, one can find the spiraling waves of a river, the reeds of the marshes, or the texture of cloth in Assyrian art.

Monumental art from the Assyrian Empire is well known since this was the focus of early archaeological investigations. Because a lot of reliefs found their way to places like the British Museum, the Louvre, and the Metropolitan Museum of Art, it's quite accessible; you don't have to go to Iraq to see them. Later digs found more intimate art, such as bronzes, gold jewelry, ivories, and furniture pieces, but a lot of this has stayed in Iraq. Some of these pieces have also been lost, thanks to the plundering of the Iraq Museum in 2003, though some items have been found on the art market and returned to Iraq.

Carved ivories were a luxury that the Assyrians really loved. Max Mallowan found a huge number at Nimrud (called the Nimrud ivories), including some fascinating and lively large-scale carvings. Many were made either outside of Assyria in Phoenicia or in Egypt or by Phoenician and Egyptian craftsmen who had relocated to Assyria. Intriguingly, when the Medes destroyed Kalhu, they had no idea that the ivory was valuable. They stripped off the gold leaf that originally covered many of the ivories and then threw the wrecked pieces into a well.

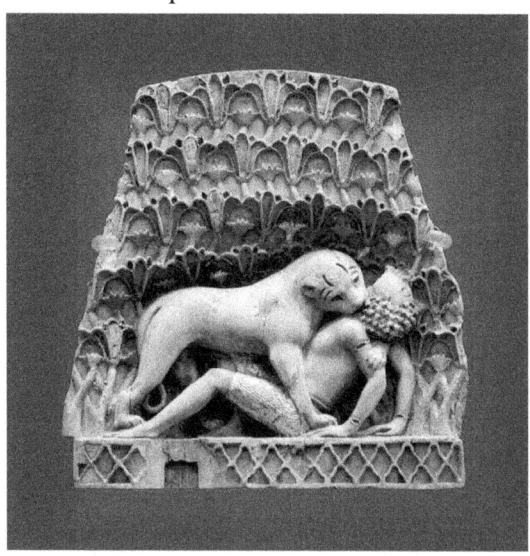

An ivory masterpiece from the palace at Kalhu.[18]

Another luxury good was glass. In the early period, it was not blown but built up around a core that could then be removed. Later on, it was cast in molds and then finished by grinding and polishing, as if it was stone.

A final typical Mesopotamian art form is the seal. In prehistory, stone amulets were pressed on clay to attest to the ownership and integrity of packages of goods. The cylinder seal, which was rolled across clay to create a rectangular panel, was developed around 3500 BCE. Its use expanded with the introduction of cuneiform script and the use of clay tablets, which could be sealed the way we would sign a letter or document.

However, when Aramaic became widely used, the cylinder seal was not so useful. Stamp seals were created, enabling the sealing of leather or papyrus rolls. Royal stamp seals show the king stabbing a lion. Cylinder seals were more likely to show a number of tiny figures, such as winged bulls, goddesses (surrounded by stars, their *melammu* or divine radiance) and gods, symbols of gods (such as the winged disk or the thunderbolt), and scenes of worship. The work on cylinder seals can be incredibly detailed. A tiny four-centimeter-high seal can show four or five separate figures.

There was another form of art that the Assyrians were experts at: the art of war. No book on the Assyrians would be complete without a mention of Assyrian military equipment and battle tactics, which were redeveloped several times to meet new conditions on the battlefield.

One of the most important weapons was the composite bow, which was a bit more than a yard long. Since it was made of different woods with different compression and release characteristics, it gave greater force to the arrow than a simple bow. Archers were usually mounted, not on a horse but on a chariot. Since a bow requires both hands, the chariot was a two-man team, with a driver to accompany the archer who did the fighting. (The archer would have been the higher one in status, as can be seen from reliefs with the king fighting from a chariot.)

Chariots were maneuverable in the flat lands of Mesopotamia. (Later, when the Assyrians started to fight in the more broken country of the Levant and the Iranian marches, they adopted the cavalry. But even at the start, they used teams, with one man controlling both horses and the other shooting.) The chariots would be used at the beginning of an engagement to smash into the enemy, weakening the line of defense and opening the opposing army's ranks up. The Assyrian infantry would then penetrate through the gaps.

Chariots continued to be upgraded throughout the Neo-Assyrian period. They were made heavier and larger so that they could carry three and, eventually, four men. By Ashurbanipal's time, they were so strong and armored that they were like horse-drawn tanks.

The Assyrians can generally be recognized on reliefs by their panoply of conical helmets. They wore mail shirts of metal plates that were arranged like fish scales on leather and a shield. The shield might be round and made of wood with a metal boss. It could be convex and made of reeds bound with leather or wooden staves, which could cover a man's legs up to the waist. Or shields could be conical; these were used mainly by the king's bodyguard.

The infantry generally used spears and pikes but had a sword or dagger for close-range fighting. Ceremonial mace heads have been found, but these were outdated by the Middle Assyrian Empire since porcelain mace heads could certainly not have been used in war; they would have smashed to bits. They must have been carried purely for ceremonial purposes, just as US Navy officers carry swords today.

Siege warfare was an Assyrian specialty, though they had no artillery and had to operate at close quarters. Reliefs show a plethora of different kinds of battering rams, siege engines, and mobile siege towers, which provided a platform for archers to shoot from, as well as a potential assault base. Palace friezes show Assyrian soldiers climbing ladders to assault the walls. In Sennacherib's palace, the siege of Lachish takes up over six hundred square feet of wall.

Sapping and tunneling were used, and diverting water channels was another frequent technique.

An Assyrian siege engine attacks a city wall.[19]

At Tell el-Duweir, the site of Lachish, there is evidence of a massive fire and an Assyrian siege ramp built of stone. Arrowheads and sling stones were left where they fell.

The cost of such a siege was very high. For the most part, the Assyrians would have tried to secure a negotiated surrender. Promises of amnesty would be made, similar to Sennacherib's offer to the Hebrews. These promises were always honored so enemies knew they could rely on being treated well if they surrendered. Then, the Assyrians would proceed to destroy the orchards, plantations, and irrigation works around the city. Trees take a long time to grow back, so the city's long-term future was at stake. Finally, the Assyrians might execute hostages—usually by impalement—publicly below the walls. Most sieges did not get this far.

Initially, being in the Assyrian army was a seasonal affair. The army could not campaign when there was agricultural work to be done, and the men had to gather at Ashur before setting out. However, the Neo-Assyrian Empire introduced a standing army, which made a huge difference to Assyria's campaigning ability. Now, the army could campaign all year, enabling long-distance operations as far away as Egypt.

Another big change in the late empire was the use of auxiliary troops from subject regions, who can be distinguished by their dress, hairstyles, and weapons in the reliefs. Slingers from Judea formed a useful contingent (remember how David killed Goliath with a slingshot?).

One style that Assyria never really adopted was naval warfare. The first use of ships dates from 694 BCE under Sennacherib, and even then, Assyria used Phoenician and Greek ships and crew. Given the rise of the Greek city-states, many of which became strong maritime powers, this would have been a major handicap had Assyria tried to expand farther west into the Mediterranean.

Taking a territory in war is one thing; holding on to it is quite another. This was where the King's Road came in. This was a postal or messenger service. Each governor was tasked with maintaining the staging posts in their provinces. This served only the state, not private travelers. All nobles had signet rings with the imperial emblem on them; a letter carrying this seal would immediately be identified as a letter requiring urgent transmission. Envoys might also be sent, particularly if the matter was too sensitive to write down, but it was an Assyrian innovation to send a letter without an envoy to get to the receiver quicker. It was slower than

USPS, but it was reliable if you had the right signet ring. Without the right stamp on the letter, though, your letter might not get taken anywhere at all.

Conclusion

The Assyrians occupy a crucial place in the history of the world. Without the Assyrians, there might not have been a Neo-Babylonian Empire or a Persian Empire. Alexander the Great might have stayed an unknown Macedonian king, and Rome might never have expanded to take over most of Europe. The very idea of an empire is one of Assyria's legacies.

While Egypt often clung to the past, Assyria managed to adapt to circumstances while always looking back at its roots for inspiration. The development of advanced accounting systems, trade enclaves, and a post office, as well as the mobility of peoples within the empire, were all new developments, and future empires benefited because of it. Assyria became a military empire due to its trading empire, the same way British imperialism grew out of the trading adventures of the East India Company.

Assyria frequently borrowed from Babylonian culture, though it retained its own distinctive language. It was also the first empire to see belonging as more important than ethnic identity. The definition of an Assyrian was quite simply someone who sacrificed to Ashur or provided goods for those sacrifices.

The truly amazing thing about Assyria, though, is that it appears to have been under the control of the same family for almost two thousand years. Compared to Sumerian history, which features incessant, discontinuous change, with cities and dynasties competing for power, Assyria was a stable and orderly empire. It identified itself as a force for order, bringing civilization and the worship of Ashur to other lands. Temples and palaces were rebuilt time and time again, but they were always on the same site and always included the original foundation inscriptions if they could be found.

When the Persian Empire was created by Cyrus, who conquered Babylon in 539, it used a different language (Elamite, not an Akkadian language). Still, the Persians copied much of their civilization from the Mesopotamian cultures. The *lamassu* flew from Assyria to the Persian capital of Persepolis, and Persian nobles collected Assyrian objets d'art.

More recently, Saddam Hussein co-opted Assyrian monuments into his own style of empire-building. Unfortunately, this made archaeological sites and museums prime targets for the opposition. There was the looting of the Iraq Museum, ISIS's destruction of the ziggurat at Kalhu, and the bulldozing of much of Nineveh. Looking at the 20th-century history of Mesopotamia, one can only conclude that the Assyrian Empire did a pretty good job of running a stable and prosperous state.

If you enjoyed this book, a review on Amazon would be greatly appreciated because it would mean a lot to hear from you.

To leave a review:
1. Open your camera app.
2. Point your mobile device at the QR code.
3. The review page will appear in your web browser.

Thanks for your support!

Here's another book by Enthralling History that you might like

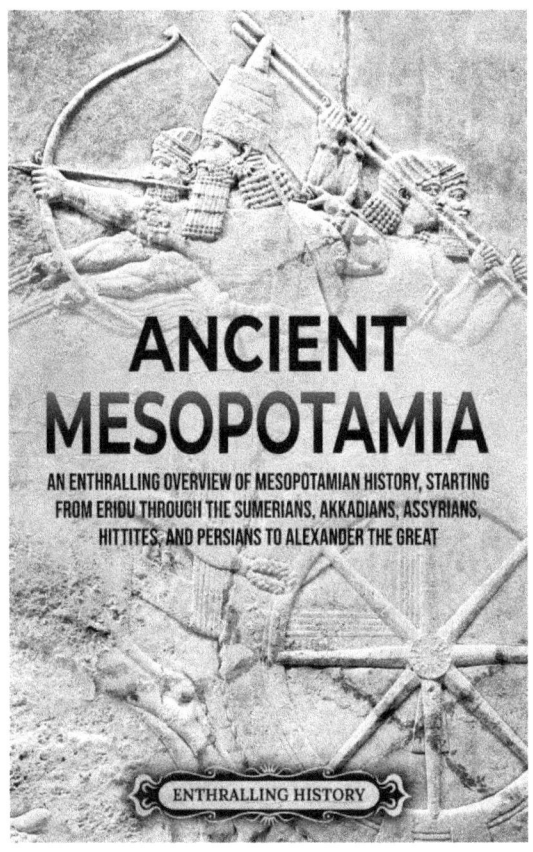

Free limited time bonus

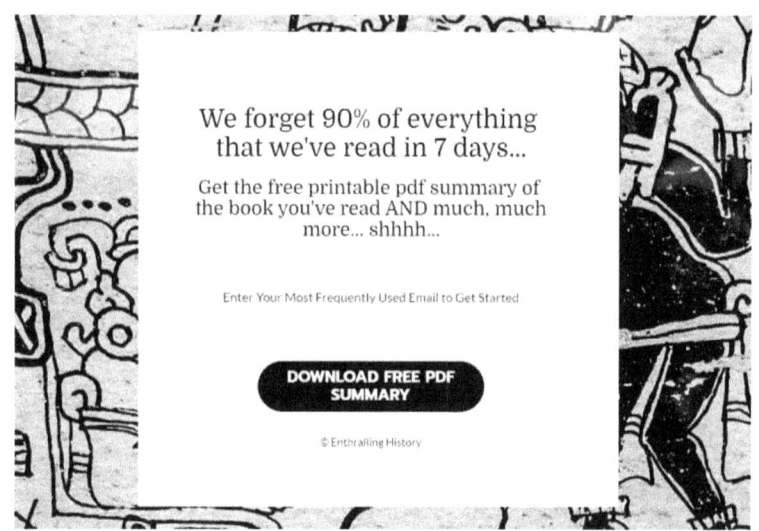

Stop for a moment. We have a free bonus set up for you. The problem is this: we forget 90% of everything that we read after 7 days. Crazy fact, right? Here's the solution: we've created a printable, 1-page pdf summary for this book that you're reading now. All you have to do to get your free pdf summary is to go to the following website: https://livetolearn.lpages.co/enthrallinghistory/

Or, Scan the QR code!

Once you do, it will be intuitive. Enjoy, and thank you!

Bibliography

Cotterell, Arthur. *The First Great Powers: Babylon and Assyria*. Hurst & Company, London, 2019.

Crawford, Harriet. *The Sumerian World*. Routledge, London and New York, 2013.

Crawford, Vaughn E; Harper, Prudence O; Pittmann, Holly. *Assyrian Reliefs and Ivories in the Metropolitan Museum of Art: Palace Reliefs of Ashurnasirpal II and Ivory Carvings from Nimrud*. Metropolitan Museum of Art, New York, 1980.

Curtis, JE and Reade, JE. *Art and Empire: Treasures from Assyria in the British Museum*. British Museum Press, London, 1995.

Düring, Bleda S. *The Imperialisation of Assyria: An Archaeological Approach*. Cambridge University Press, Cambridge, 2020.

Elayi, Josette. *Sargon II, King of Assyria*. SBL Press, Atlanta, 2017.

Elayi, Josette. *Esarhaddon, King of Assyria*. Lockwood Press, Columbus, Georgia, 2023.

Elayi, Josette. *Sennacherib, King of Assyria*. SBL Press, Atlanta, 2018.

Frahm, Eckart. *A Companion to Assyria*. Wiley Blackwell, Malden MA, 2017.

Frahm, Eckart. *Assyria: The Rise and Fall of the World's First Empire*. Basic Books, New York, 2023.

Kramer, Samuel Noah. *The Sumerians: Their History, Culture and Character*. University of Chicago Press, Chicago, 1963.

Melville, Sarah C. *The Campaigns of Sargon II, King of Assyria, 721-705 BC*. University of Oklahoma Press, Norman, Oklahoma, 2016.

Radner, Karen. *Ancient Assyria: A Very Short Introduction.* Oxford University Press, Oxford, 2015.

Image Sources

[1] https://commons.wikimedia.org/wiki/File:Artist%E2%80%99s_impression_of_Assyrian_palaces_from_The_Monuments_of_Nineveh_by_Sir_Austen_Henry_Layard,_1853.jpg

[2] *Goran tek-en, CC BY-SA 4.0 <https://creativecommons.org/licenses/by-sa/4.0>, via Wikimedia Commons;* https://commons.wikimedia.org/wiki/File:N-Mesopotamia_and_Syria_english.svg

[3] *Hardnfast, CC BY 3.0 <https://creativecommons.org/licenses/by/3.0>, via Wikimedia Commons;* https://commons.wikimedia.org/wiki/File:Ancient_ziggurat_at_Ali_Air_Base_Iraq_2005.jpg

[4] https://commons.wikimedia.org/wiki/File:Sargon_of_Akkad_(1936).jpg

[5] https://commons.wikimedia.org/wiki/File:Gudea_of_Lagash_Girsu.jpg

[6] *Jononmac46, CC BY-SA 3.0 <https://creativecommons.org/licenses/by-sa/3.0>, via Wikimedia Commons;* https://commons.wikimedia.org/wiki/File:Assyrian_lions.png)

[7] *Hammurabi, CC BY 3.0 <https://creativecommons.org/licenses/by/3.0>, via Wikimedia Commons;* https://commons.wikimedia.org/wiki/File:P1050763_Louvre_code_Hammurabi_face_rwk.JPG

[8] https://commons.wikimedia.org/wiki/File:Iraq;_Nimrud_-_Assyria,_Lamassu%27s_Guarding_Palace_Entrance.jpg

[9] *Osama Shukir Muhammed Amin FRCP(Glasg), CC BY-SA 4.0 <https://creativecommons.org/licenses/by-sa/4.0>, via Wikimedia Commons;* https://commons.wikimedia.org/wiki/File:Ashurnasirpal_II_performs_religious_rituals_before_the_sacred_tree._From_Nimrud,_Iraq._865-860_BCE._British_Museum.jpg

[10] https://commons.wikimedia.org/wiki/File:Tell_Ahmar,_mural_palacio_rey_Tiglatpileser_audiencia_sicglo_VIII.jpg

[11] Osama Shukir Muhammed Amin FRCP(Glasg), CC BY-SA 4.0 <https://creativecommons.org/licenses/by-sa/4.0>, via Wikimedia Commons; https://commons.wikimedia.org/wiki/File:Tiglath-pileser_III,_an_alabaster_bas-relief_from_the_king%27s_central_palace_at_Nimrud,_Mesopotamia..JPG

[12] https://commons.wikimedia.org/wiki/File:Reconstructed_Model_of_Palace_of_Sargon_at_Khosrabad_1905.jpg

[13] Timo Roller, CC BY 3.0 <https://creativecommons.org/licenses/by/3.0>, via Wikimedia Commons; https://commons.wikimedia.org/wiki/File:Sanherib-tr-1271.jpg

[14] Photograph: Anthony Huan Text: George Smith in 1871 (Public domain), CC BY-SA 2.0 <https://creativecommons.org/licenses/by-sa/2.0>, via Wikimedia Commons; https://commons.wikimedia.org/wiki/File:Rassam_cylinder_with_translation_of_the_First_Assyrian_Conquest_of_Egypt,_643_BCE.jpg

[15] https://commons.wikimedia.org/wiki/File:Ashur_god.jpg

[16] Sailko, CC BY 3.0 <https://creativecommons.org/licenses/by/3.0>, via Wikimedia Commons; https://commons.wikimedia.org/wiki/File:Ishtar_on_an_Akkadian_seal.jpg

[17] Allan Gluck, CC BY 4.0 <https://creativecommons.org/licenses/by/4.0>, via Wikimedia Commons; https://commons.wikimedia.org/wiki/File:Assyrian_Relief_of_the_Banquet_of_Ashurbanipal_From_Nineveh_Gypsum_N_Palace_British_Museum_01.jpg

[18] British Museum, CC BY-SA 3.0 <https://creativecommons.org/licenses/by-sa/3.0>, via Wikimedia Commons; https://commons.wikimedia.org/wiki/File:Inlaid_and_gilded_panel_-_WA_127412_-_British_Museum.JPG

[19] Osama Shukir Muhammed Amin FRCP(Glasg), CC BY-SA 4.0 <https://creativecommons.org/licenses/by-sa/4.0>, via Wikimedia Commons; https://commons.wikimedia.org/wiki/File:Assyrian_siege-engine_attacking_the_city_wall_of_Lachish,_part_of_the_ascending_assaulting_wave._Detail_of_a_wall_relief_dating_back_to_the_reign_of_Sennacherib,_700-692_BCE._From_Nineveh,_Iraq,_currently_housed_in_the_British_Museum.jpg

www.ingramcontent.com/pod-product-compliance
Lightning Source LLC
Chambersburg PA
CBHW070339010526
44107CB00004B/552